THE SEED
A Leader's Growth Path

THE SEED
A Leader's Growth Path

Milverton Ojegun

Trendy Publishing LLC

THE SEED...A Leader's Growth Path

Copyright©2014 by Milverton Ojegun.

All rights reserved. No portion of this book may be reproduced, stored in a retrieval system, or transmitted in any form, or by any means - electronic, mechanical, photocopy, recording, scanning, or other without the prior written permission of the publisher.

Request for information on this title should be addressed to
Milverton Ojegun
6061 Ducketts Lane, Elkridge MD 21075
Email: eojegun@yahoo.com
+1240 381 1710 (USA)

Unless otherwise indicated, all Scripture quotations are from the Holy Bible: King James Version (KJV), New American Standard, New King James Version, Amplified, American Standard Bible, The Message, Aramaic Bible in Plain English, of the Holy Bible.
All Rights Reserved

Library of Congress Cataloging-in-Publication Data

Milverton Ojegun
THE SEED...A Leader's Growth Path
ISBN-13: 978-0-990-82340-7 (Paperback)
ISBN-10: 0-9908-2340-7 (Paperback)
1. Inspiration - Non-fiction 1. Title
Library of Congress Control Number: 2014951181

Edited by Winnie Aduayi
Designed by Trendy Graphics Dept.

Published in Dallas Texas by Trendy Publishing. A registered trademark of Trendy Communications llc. www.trendyafrica.com info@trendyafrica.com

Printed in USA

Dedication

To God Almighty without whom NOTHING WILL EVER BE POSSIBLE.

Acknowledgements

This work is a result of opportunities made possible by God to serve in His Vineyard. It is a collection of learnings from the best, and staying in His presence in other to remain focused on the call to leadership.

Success cannot be achieved without helping hands. I want to acknowledge all members of Jesus House Elkridge for continuously encouraging me as a Leader.

To my lovely wife, Mreta for standing by me through thick and thin, praying and encouraging me, as my number one supporter in chief, and taking good care of our boys and I. I will always love and cherish you. Thank you for making me look good. To our boys: Tega, Rume, and Garen, for making me work hard, and for seeing me as your superhero, I love you all.

To Winifred Aduayi, my great and excellent editor, thank you for putting this book together and spending so much time to make sure it comes out as the best.

Many thanks to the entire leadership team and congregation of Jesus House Elkridge, who I have been priviledged to work with and share the awesome revelations God blesses me with.

To all my friends, too numerous to mention. I salute you all.

Finally, I acknowledge God Almighty that planted and watered the seed, and who ensures I stay on the right path.

Milverton Ojegun

Contents

Introduction..10

PROLOGUE:
Faith Workout..14

CHAPTER ONE:
The Battle Within..18

CHAPTER TWO:
The Way of the Ant...34

CHAPTER THREE:
The Makeover..54

CHAPTER FOUR:
Unrestricted Access...73

CHAPTER FIVE:
The Power of Imagination..89

CHAPTER SIX:
The Race Factor...98

CHAPTER SEVEN:
The Conversation..106

CHAPTER EIGHT:
The Path to Greatness: The Seed............................118

CHAPTER NINE:
Non-Disclosure Agreement...130

CHAPTER TEN:
When the Nations Are Raging..141

CHAPTER ELEVEN:
The Mind Game...150

CHAPTER TWELVE:
Beyond Knowledge..157

CHAPTER THIRTEEN:
The Rear View Mirror..166

EPILOGUE:
The Power of Gratitude..173

Introduction

Whether life is going well for you or collapsing right before your eyes, the truth remains that we all want to grow beyond where we are, and be able to sustain that growth. We want to excel in life; we want to know God more; we want to be better spouses and parents; we want to excel more in all that we do. Whether we believe it or not, God, our creator, put something deep down in us that evokes the desire to grow, because we, ourselves, are a seed that God planted, watered, watches over, and expects to continue to grow, to become richly fruitful and replenish His earth. Hence, we were born for better than this, and designed to live at a higher level than where we are.

A man in Jerusalem had been crippled for thirty-eight years. He spent every day of his life lying by the pool of Bethesda, hoping for a miracle (John 5). This man had a deep-seated, lingering disorder nonetheless. This problem affected all that he was, his self-image, and all that he desired to be. Just like the man lying by the pool, some of us sit back for years, waiting for a miracle to happen that will make everything better.

However, when Jesus saw the man lying there, He asked a simple, straightforward question: Do you want to be made well? I have never ceased to be amazed by the man's response. He began by listing all of his excuses for still being in that position for thirty-eight years, "I'm alone, I have no one to help me...." Little wonder he had not been healed, nor his situation changed. Jesus looked at him, and must have shook His head and said, in simple language, "If you are serious about getting well, about getting ahead, if you really want to get out of this mess, then get up off the ground, pick up your bed and be on your way". Thus, Jesus gave the man the seed, what he does with that seed, was entirely up to him; but thank God, the man obeyed, he got up, picked up his bed and got on his way.

What you do with your situation matters; you can sit there and make excuses all day, or you can get up and follow through with your life. You are the King's child, and you have an inheritance, it is your right as a child of God, but you cannot receive that inheritance by doing nothing and making excuses. God is a God of order, not confusion; therefore, there is order in the kingdom, and when you are out of order, you can easily miss the Father's blessing, and then lose your inheritance.

Mathew 25:34
Then the King will say to those on His right, "come, you who are blessed by my father; take your inheritance, the kingdom prepared for you since the creation of the world"

This book, 'The Seed: A Leader's Growth Path', is very critical at this point in our lives, as I believe that God is calling on us all to have a full concept and purpose of the kingdom. It is very important that we understand certain principles in order for us to have a better knowledge of how we are to pursue our desires, or to get the inheritance He has created for us. One of the things we must not forget is that God knows what is ahead; there are things we must avoid, and there are things we must follow to be on His right.

"Then the king said to those on his right". Who are those on his right? Being on His right gives you the key into Kingdom dominion.

Genesis 1:26-27
Then God said let us make man in our image, in our likeness, and let them rule (have dominion) over the fish of the sea and the birds of the air, over the livestock, over all the earth and over all creatures that move along the ground. So God created man in his own image, in the image of God he created him; male and female he created them.

I want you to understand that you are a reflection of God's very image and created to act like Him. You were not an accident waiting to happen. It was a conscious effort from God to create you as He is. When God put together The Kingdom, certain principles were laid down on how to operate in the kingdom, in order to get maximum benefit of the kingdom. God rules the kingdom, and the inheritance has two parts: here on earth, and in heaven; but we will focus on the earthly inheritance. Every Will has some terms and conditions, and certain principles must be followed before the inheritance can be released. The purpose of this book is to uncover those multi-faceted principles for you to be on God's right, and for you to confidently live at your full operational status, to get the maximum benefit of your Father's kingdom.

Luke 12:32
Fear not, little flock; for it is your Father's good pleasure to give you the kingdom.

Prologue

Faith Workout
"Faith is a muscle that needs to be exercised"

The Bible says, in this world you will have tribulations, troubles, sequestration, marital issues, children issues, money issues, job issues – people will let you down, and you will let some people down, but "I will never leave you nor forsake you, because I deposited something great in you when you were created".

Faith is what we need to overcome sequestration. Faith is what we need to overcome fiscal cliff; it is what you need to breath, period.

I discovered that everyone has inbuilt faith that comes from the Creator. Every product was designed to serve a unique purpose in the eyes of the manufacturer, and there is always something the manufacturer adds to his product, something called manufacturer warranty. It may mean that if you use this product as required, and you have an issue within several months of getting it, you can send it back to the manufacturer and it will be replaced at no cost.

So, when God created us there was a manufacturer warranty, but this one works a little differently from a physical product. I discovered by revelation that this warranty is called faith. Every believer has been given a measure, the same measure of the God-kind of faith.

Ephesians 2:8
For by grace are ye saved through faith; and that not of yourselves: IT IS THE GIFT OF GOD.

Romans 12:3
According as GOD HATH DEALT TO EVERY MAN the measure of faith.

Notice something in the above scripture: we don't try to get faith; we already have a measure of faith. Everyone was given a measure, something to start with, and something to make reference to. The measure of faith can be increased, but it is up to you and I to increase our faith, not God. We know the bible says, "Faith comes by hearing and hearing the word of God" Yes it's true, but what do you do after you hear the Word of GOD? What do you do with what you have heard repeatedly? If you hear and don't 'do', nothing will happen.

> **Faith is a Muscle, if you don't exercise your muscles they will become weak.**

Faith workout is about the doing aspect. Faith is a Muscle, if you don't exercise your muscles they will become weak. Each time you exercise the muscle called Faith, it grows and increases in strength, but when you don't exercise the faith muscle, it reduces in strength. It is up to you what you do with the measure of Faith God gave you. When last did you take your faith for a workout?

One day Jesus wanted to teach His disciples this principle of faith work out, and He did it as thus:

Mathew 14:13-21
When Jesus heard what had happened, he withdrew by boat privately to a solitary place. Hearing of this, the crowds followed him on foot from the towns. When Jesus landed and saw a large crowd, he had compassion on them and healed their sick. As evening approached, the disciples came to him and said, This is a remote place, and it's already getting late. Send the crowds away, so they can go to the villages and buy themselves some food. Jesus replied, They do not need to go away. You give them something to eat. We have here only five loaves of bread and two fish, they answered. Bring them here to me," he said. And he directed the people to sit down on the grass. Taking the five loaves and the two fish and looking up to heaven, he gave thanks and broke the loaves. Then he gave them to the disciples, and the disciples gave them to the people. They all ate and were satisfied, and the disciples picked up twelve basketfuls of broken pieces that were left over. The number of those who ate was about five thousand men, besides women and children.

Something terrible had just happened to John the Baptist: he was just beheaded and the people were discouraged. Has something happened, that you feel discouraged? Did you hear news that depressed you? When Jesus heard that news, HE WENT TO THE FAITH GYM FOR A WORKOUT. After the work out, Jesus decided to allow His disciples do a workout of their own immediately after He showed them what can be achieved. He TOOK THE DISCIPLES TO THE GYM FOR A WORKOUT. There will be situations in life where you need to workout on your faith muscles.

In Matthew 14:22-36 (Read),

He told Peter, *"You of Little Faith"*, while in **Matthew 8:5-13,** He told the centurion that he had such a great faith. Faith grows through exercise. Step into the Gym of life and exercise that muscle called faith.

Chapter One

The Battle Within

"I have discovered this principle that when I want to do what is right, I inevitably do what is wrong" Romans 7:21

Suddenly there is a loud banging on the door of the brick house. Once he opens the door Stephen's life will never be the same. It's like the chilling phone call you get in the middle of the night or the unexpected rap at your front door... an unannounced visit from the devil himself.
The visitor, Saul, an evil man known for killing Christians, bursts in without being invited, and orders his followers to seize Stephen and have him stoned to death. Stephen died by the stone, and the Apostles witnessed it all. Fear and uncertainty enveloped the hearts of these God-loving men, none of them could preach the truth to Saul to change his heart, and the battles raged relentlessly within their hearts, as to what to do, or how to live their lives here on; either to live by Paul's rules and stay alive, or to live by God's rules and risk getting killed by Saul. The battle within to make the right choice was fierce.

The Battle goes on and on, inside us as believers. It is the struggles we constantly face as we try to do what is right, or live right. Battles within are never won as easily; it is often won as a result of strong mental effort: thinking clearly, courageously and confidently. No one ever waltzed his way out of a battle like a lazy slug.

Saul, now Apostle Paul, who eventually became a Christian, preached to by the resurrected Christ, has this to say...

2 Corinthians 11:21-33 (NIV)
To my shame I admit that we were too weak for that! Whatever anyone else dares to boast about—I am speaking as a fool—I also dare to boast about. Are they Hebrews? So am I. Are they Israelites? So am I. Are they Abraham's descendants? So am I. Are they servants of Christ? (I am out of my mind to talk like this.) I am more. I have worked much harder, been in prison more frequently, been flogged more severely, and been exposed to death again and again. Five times I received from the Jews the forty lashes minus one. Three times I was beaten with rods, once I was pelted with stones, three times I was shipwrecked, I spent a night and a day in the open sea, I have been constantly on the move. I have been in danger from rivers, in danger from bandits, in danger from my fellow Jews, in danger from Gentiles; in danger in the city, in danger in the country, in danger at sea; and in danger from false believers. I have labored and toiled and have often gone without sleep; I have known hunger and thirst and have often gone without food; I have been cold and naked. Besides everything else, I face daily the pressure of my concern for all the churches. Who is weak, and I do not feel weak? Who is led into sin, and I do not inwardly burn? If I must boast, I will

boast of the things that show my weakness. The God and Father of the Lord Jesus, who is to be praised forever, knows that I am not lying. In Damascus the governor under King Aretas had the city of the Damascenes guarded in order to arrest me. But I was lowered in a basket from a window in the wall and slipped through his hands.

Here, we see that Paul was able to withstand any thing that came his way; he was able to suffer all these for the gospel, and he was able to beat any and almost all external forces. However, there was one enemy that he could not handle by what he had learnt alone, and that was the battle within. Thus, he came to the conclusion that the battle within is stronger than the battle without. The battle within eats like cancer, if not properly taken care of.

...the battle within is won by not leaning on your own understanding, your own ideologies, your own rules and regulations.

He summarized this in **Romans 7:21-25**
I have discovered this principle of life that when I want to do what is right, I inevitably do what is wrong. I love God's law with all my heart. But there is another power within me that is at war with my mind. This power makes me a slave to the sin that is still within me. Oh, what a miserable person I am! Who will free me from this life that is dominated by sin and death? Thank God! The answer is in Jesus Christ our Lord. So you see how it is: In my mind I really want to obey God's law, but because of my sinful nature I am a slave to sin.

Paul is saying that the answer is in Jesus. If we want to fight the battle within, we must starve the flesh with the grace of God, which is sufficient and abounds to us unto every good work.

Romans 8: 12-13
Therefore, brothers and sisters, we have an obligation, but it is not to the flesh, to live according to it. For if you live according to the flesh, you will die; but if by the Spirit you put to death the misdeeds of the body, you will live.

The battle within for me may not necessarily be the battle within for you. What battles are you fighting within? What struggles are you facing? Perhaps yours is a combination of battle within and without. What wolves have you been feeding over the years, empowering them for the next twenty years? What struggles are you fighting within; do you still get angry easily? Do you still lash out, or fire back? Is the wolf rising up every time you are reminded of the law?

The battle within must be won by trusting Jesus; the battle within is won by not leaning on your own understanding, your own ideologies, your own rules and regulations. The battle within is won by accepting Jesus and staying committed. The battle within is won by not staying on the floor when you fall, but by rising and asking God to help you.

****

The Trial

"We have examined this, and it is true. So hear it and apply it to yourself" Job 5:27

Some of us must have been in a court setting before, and have an idea of what goes on in a court, or we have seen movies that has court settings in them. However, before we begin with our proceedings, there are some terms that we may have become familiar with, which I believe has lost its meaning over the years, but are important.

When God is going to do something wonderful, He begins with difficulty. If it is going to be something very wonderful, He begins with impossibility!"

"Christianity has not been tried and found wanting; it has been found difficult and not tried." -Gilbert K. Chesterton

I dare say that when Difficulty gets tougher, and then graduates, it becomes 'an impossibility' in the eyes of man.

Jeremiah 29:11(AMP)
For I know the thoughts and plans that I have for you, says the Lord, thoughts and plans for welfare and peace and not for evil, to give you hope in your final outcome.

One thing we must be aware of is that God is thinking of us. 'My thoughts' means, when God created you, there are things He already put in place because of you; there are line items that has been strategized just to lead you and you alone. No man has the same finger print as you do, so you are one of a kind.

- His plans of welfare and peace has to do with your well being, and not being troubled; you are able to sleep peacefully without allowing what you are faced with to

overwhelm you, or discourage you.
- God's plan is not for evil to befall us, it is not waiting for us to fall into trouble; no father will see a ditch in front of his baby and allow the baby to crawl to that ditch. Rather, he will create a barrier around that ditch so that evil does not befall the child.
- A hope and final outcome has to do with our expectations, knowing fully well that no matter how dark the night is, morning will always show up.

Therefore, when we are in a trial period, evidence will be brought forward, accusing fingers will be pointed at you. The enemy will require maximum sentence, and if you don't know your rights or entitlements, guess what happens:

Proverbs 10:21 *The lips of the righteous nourish many, but fools die for lack of judgment.*

Isaiah 5:13 *Therefore my people will go into exile for lack of understanding; their men of rank will die of hunger and their masses will be parched with thirst.*

Hosea 8:12 *I wrote for them the many things of my law, but they regarded them as something alien.*

What do you plead? At the beginning of the case, you will be read the charges, and asked how you plead: guilty or not guilty. It is left for you to accept the situation and serve the sentence, or fight against it and defend yourself with Jesus as your advocate. Some of us are serving sentences right now, because we did not have understanding of the law, we regarded many things in the law as alien, as something that does not have to do with us.

Some of us are in the middle of a trial period right now, and you are wondering, do I make a plea bargain? A plea bargain is a negotiation in which the defendant agrees to enter a plea of guilty to a lesser charge, and the prosecutor agrees to drop a more serious charge. Some opt for a plea bargain, because we do not know our rights.

Therefore, before you plead your case, here is something we need to know; some of the things we need to digest, comprehend, and make part of our spirits and thoughts:

The Covenant of God with His people is a legal contract, and His protection and provision are in the terms of the contract on His part.
Two important things in that covenant are 'Protection and Provision': protection in times of danger, protection in times of calamity. If prayers are taken away from our daily activities, danger is always eminent.

Isaiah 54:10
Though the mountains be shaken and the hills be removed, yet my unfailing love for you will not be shaken, nor my covenant of peace be removed," says the LORD, who has compassion on you.

Jeremiah 31:36
Only if these decrees vanish from my sight," declares the LORD, "will the descendants of Israel ever cease to be a nation before me.

God has adopted us; it is possible to have a child you didn't plan for, but you never adopt a child you did not plan for. Keep that in mind always, it makes it much easier to plead your case more effectively.

Going through the Old Testament you will discover that many writers used the format of pleading with God, as if arguing a case in a court of law:

David said in **Psalm 140:12** - *I know and rest in confidence upon it that the Lord will maintain the cause of the afflicted, and will secure justice for the poor and needy [of His believing children]*

Job 23:4 - *I would state my case before him and fill my mouth with arguments.*

Job 5:27 - *We have examined this, and it is true. So hear it and apply it to yourself.*

****

The Right to Remain Silent

As we learnt earlier, the trial period is a time when we lay our case and argue our position before God, as in a law court. It is also a time when we stand on the promises of God, and on the covenant that God has for us as His adopted children. We arm ourselves with all the attributes and all the access that God has given us as His children.

More so, the trial period is a time when we are offensive, and at the same time defensive, like David, who was placed at the defense stand, yet was still offensive in terms of the prayers he prayed against the people that wanted to take his life, or see him perish.

What we have looked at: defending, being offensive, declaring your case, saying you are not guilty, etc., can be summed up in the things you say, and the things you do in the court of law.

We must, as a necessity, do all these, and be satisfied that we have done all that we need to do, before the judge asks to adjourn the case or trial which brings me to the above sub-title: The Right to Remain Silent. Here we will try to answer the question: When do you exercise your right to remain silent?

Luke 22:39-46
Jesus went out as usual to the Mount of Olives, and his disciples followed him. On reaching the place, he said to them, "Pray that you will not fall into temptation." He withdrew about a stone's throw beyond them, knelt down and prayed, "Father, if you are willing, take this cup from me; yet not my will, but yours be done." An angel from heaven appeared to him and strengthened him. And being in anguish, he prayed more earnestly, and his sweat was like drops of blood falling to the ground.
  When he rose from prayer and went back to the disciples, he found them asleep, exhausted from sorrow. "Why are you sleeping?" he asked them. Get up and pray so that you will not fall into temptation.

We see Jesus trying to show them a pattern of what you need to do before, during, and after a trial. The first thing He told them was to pray, and when He came back

He repeated the same thing.

Note that:
-The allegations had already been placed on Him. Decisions had been made concerning what they wanted to do to Jesus.
- The enemy had made allegations and decisions before He will be taken to the trial
- The enemy had already planned what they wanted to do before this time
- Jesus went out as usual to pray, before the physical trial.
- What He was doing at the time of prayer was to lay His own side of the argument before God. He was presenting His case as He ought to, before God
- He was feeling His mouth, like Job, with arguments. Remember that though He is God, He came in the form of man, He still suffered what we suffered, He still went through pain and temptation, he was every bit a man with all the attributes, but suffered without loosing His attributes as God.
- He told them to go on the offensive, "Pray that you will not fall into temptation". As simple as this statement is, it is very powerful. It means a lot.

It means "Pray before you begin to face issues at home, especially in your marriage, pray before your company plans to downsize and your boss has you in mind as the one to let go. Pray before your children decide it is okay to be gay, etc. Pray while you are still focused, while you are still composed, while better prepared, and while you can still encourage yourself in the Lord. It means

Pray when you still have the strength to pray. It means pray to equip yourself, your family, and your generation.

Temptation is the desire to perform an action that one may enjoy immediately or in the short term, but will probably later regret for various reasons: legal, social, psychological (including feeling guilt), health-related, economic, etc. In the context of religion, temptation is the inclination to sin.

In other words, temptation may mean entering into a plea bargain for you to accept lesser charges, if you plead guilty; instead of 10 years, you will spend 5 years. It might look tempting at that time, because you didn't know the law, or lacked understanding. If you can manipulate some figures, you will get enough money to celebrate Christmas. If you can hold back a little of your commitments to God then this Christmas will be the best Christmas ever, after all heaven helps those who helps themselves *(Just for the record, Heaven has nothing to do with those who help themselves, rather helps those who cannot help themselves)*

He withdrew some distance to pray. There will always be time that we must withdraw from the activities of life to pray. Withdraw from the hustling and bustling to seek God, to defend your case, or counter what the enemy has for you.

Luke 22:47-48
While he was still speaking, a crowd came up, and the man who was called Judas, one of the Twelve, was leading them.

He approached Jesus to kiss him, but Jesus asked him, "Judas, are you betraying the Son of Man with a kiss?"

It is possible for the enemy to come right after you finish that prayer; right after you finish that anointing service. It is possible for you to feel terrible, instead of feel better after you've been prayed for about that illness. I tell people, though you were in a deliverance session that does not stop the devil from coming back. The reason being that the devil wants to know if you actually know what your covenant is, or if you even have an understanding of who you are as a child of God.

Luke 22:66-68
At daybreak the council of the elders of the people, both the chief priests and the teachers of the law, met together, and Jesus was led before them. "If you are the Messiah," they said, "tell us." Jesus answered, "If I tell you, you will not believe me, and if I asked you, you would not answer.

Jesus is before the Chief Priest and Teachers of the Law. If you don't know the law, what is going to happen to you? Ignorance is not an excuse in any court of law

Verses 69-71, Jesus answered, *"If I tell you, you will not believe me, and if I asked you, you would not answer. But from now on, the Son of Man will be seated at the right hand of the mighty God. They all asked, "Are you then the Son of God?"*
He replied, "You say that I am. Then they said, "Why do we need any more testimony? We have heard it from his own lips."

Finally Jesus came to some type of trial; a pre-trial. He was placed before them and questions were asked, and He began to answer them accordingly. He answered the most important question they needed to know, and also to remind God that his Son is on the witness stand.

My question to you is "whose son or daughter are you when in the witness stand?" Do you realize that you have the privilege of a son or daughter of the most high? If we can answer these questions correctly, then we can be still and see the salvation of God. Jesus had prepared Himself, aligning Himself with the covenant and His right. He had an understanding of where they were going, because he had gone out to pray before the trial.

It is important to understand that the right to remain silent is a legal right recognized, explicitly or by convention, in many of the world's legal systems. The right covers a number of issues centered on the right of the accused, or the defendant, to refuse to comment or provide an answer when questioned, either prior to or during legal proceedings in a court of law.

I want us to define two very important words in the contest of this message, 'Right' and 'Silence.'
Right: Rights are entitlements (not) to perform certain actions, or (not) to be in certain states; or entitlements that others (not) perform certain actions or (not) be in certain states. Rights dominate modern understandings of what actions are permissible and which institutions are just. Rights structure the form of governments, the content of laws, and the shape of morality as it is currently perceived. To accept a set of rights is to approve a

distribution of freedom and authority, and so to endorse a certain view of what may, must, and must not be done.

Silence: Silence is sincerity, stillness of mind. It brings satisfaction; it makes you Strong. Silence creates solutions and inner strength; and more often than not, silence erases all doubts.

Luke 23:1-9
Then the whole assembly rose and led him off to Pilate. And they began to accuse him, saying, "We have found this man subverting our nation. He opposes payment of taxes to Caesar and claims to be Messiah, a king." So Pilate asked Jesus, "Are you the king of the Jews?" "You have said so," Jesus replied. Then Pilate announced to the chief priests and the crowd, "I find no basis for a charge against this man." But they insisted, "He stirs up the people all over Judea by his teaching. He started in Galilee and has come all the way here." On hearing this, Pilate asked if the man was a Galilean. When he learned that Jesus was under Herod's jurisdiction, he sent him to Herod, who was also in Jerusalem at that time. When Herod saw Jesus, he was greatly pleased, because for a long time he had been wanting to see him. From what he had heard about him, he hoped to see him perform a sign of some sort. He plied him with many questions, but Jesus gave him no answer.

Jesus exercised his rights to remain silent, and He was also calm; he was still, as He knew who His Father is.

Psalm 46:10
He says, *"Be still, and know that I am God; I will be exalted among the nations, I will be exalted in the earth."*

Exodus 14:10-12

And when Pharaoh drew nigh, the children of Israel lifted up their eyes, and, behold, the Egyptians marched after them; and they were sore afraid: and the children of Israel cried out unto the LORD. And they said unto Moses, Because there were no graves in Egypt, hast thou taken us away to die in the wilderness? wherefore hast thou dealt thus with us, to carry us forth out of Egypt? Is not this the word that we did tell thee in Egypt, saying, Let us alone, that we may serve the Egyptians? For it had been better for us to serve the Egyptians, than that we should die in the wilderness.

It is clear here that the Israelites were prepared to enter a plea bargain when they saw the horses coming after them. They were prepared to suffer more, than to see themselves die in the wilderness.

Have you come to the point where you have prayed and fasted, pulled down, and destroyed every attack thinkable concerning that situation? Have you told God that if He can deliver you from this issue, you will offer thanksgiving and celebrate Him?
Yet, it looks like help is nowhere to be found after you have prayed. It is true that the bible says pray until your joy is full, but I tell you, a time will come when you need to exercise the right to be still; a time to remain silent, and just let God do what He wants to do.

Exodus 14:13-14

And Moses said unto the people, Fear ye not, stand still, and see the salvation of the LORD, which he will shew to you to day: for the Egyptians whom ye have seen to day, ye shall see them again no more for ever. The LORD shall fight for you, and ye shall hold your peace.

For Moses, an old chapter was about to be closed and a new chapter is about to be opened. The year is rounding up, the old is rounding up and the new is about to emerge. We will defend our cause. We will fill our mouths with arguments. We will pull down every activities of the enemy, but we will be sensitive to exercise our right to remain silent. Our right to remain silent is more like prayer, is more like communication; you have spoken enough, and then allow God to speak. Our right to remain silent is not a time for us to sit down and say, "I have finished praying, let me relax now". Our right to remain silent is allowing God to act on what you have prayed for. It is a continuous process.

Have you discovered that sometimes you pray for so long and it looks like nothing is happening, but just when you are tired of repeating the same prayer points and stop that suddenly things start happening? Then, from when things start happening, you suddenly discover that you have more energy to pray. That point when you stopped talking, you started allowing God do what He wants to do; that is the time you exercised your right to remain silent.

Psalm 46:10
He says, *"Be still, and know that I am God; I will be exalted among the nations, I will be exalted in the earth."*

Chapter Two

The Way of the Ant

"Four things on earth are small, yet they are extremely wise"
Proverbs 30:24

David put on his slippers and worn robe, and wandered toward the field to tend to his father's sheep. He stumbled along the rocky path to where a cliff edge gave an unobstructed view of the entire field. Blackbirds unfurled their long, graceful wings, floating effortlessly in flocks from cliff to cliff. Little black Ants moving in such strict order, carrying tiny white things on their backs. The family of sheep grazed, the females nursing their babes, the males strolled around, as they nibbled on vegetation, while David filled their drinking containers with water, and wondered at the creativity and life lessons nature offers daily.

Often times you see in the scriptures certain animals, used in the bible to help us visualize the concept of God and how God sees certain things, or how He seeks to encourage us.

We see God use the eagle for so many things that include

strength, vision etc. We see God also use the lion to signify strength, power, or boldness.

Proverbs 30:24-28
Four things on earth are small, yet they are extremely wise: Ants are creatures of little strength, yet they store up their food in the summer; hyraxes are creatures of little power, yet they make their home in the crags; locusts have no king, yet they advance together in ranks; a lizard can be caught with the hand, yet it is found in kings' palaces.

In other words, we don't have any excuses not to live in dominion. We don't have any excuses not to live a holy life. We don't have any excuses not to be the best that God wants us to be. We don't have any excuses not to achieve greatness from where we are right now.

Here, we will look at one of the four things on earth that are small, yet extremely wise. The Ant:

The ant is so small that it has only three letters. The ant is an insect that people over look; it can be stepped on and viewed as having no potential. How is something that is so small, yet be so wise? Not just wise, but extremely wise. They store up their food in the summer, means that there must be something they do that is different from what other insects or animals do.

The Ants never allow their size to affect them: they are so small, but their dreams are very big. The ant is so small that what it carries is also small, but is able to sustain them during the winter. What this means is a total dependency on God.

In 1Samuel 17, we see a young man, David, who had no hope of becoming a warrior. Never was enlisted in the army, because he was so young and probably too skinny, and so nobody looked at him twice; but while he did his menial job tending the sheep, he had an encounter with a lion and a bear. These are two wild animals that had the ability and capacity to tear him apart and kill him, but some how God delivered him from both of them.

Look at the odds against David: there were 8 sons, three made it to the army, 5 did not, and he was the youngest of them all.

Have you ever been in situations where you look at some things and say this will never happen to me, because the odds are just too much? Did we look at the physical and just come to the conclusion to forget about going after what we want?

Eliab, the eldest son of Jesse, and the older brother of King David, was apparently tall and had fair features, but lacked the proper heart to be king of Israel (1 Samuel 16:7) *"Do not consider his appearance or his height...the Lord looks at the heart."*

Abinadab (Vs. 8) *Then Jesse called Abinadab and had him pass in front of Samuel. But Samuel said, "The LORD has not chosen this one either.*

Shammah(Vs. 9-11) *Jesse then had Shammah pass by, but Samuel said, Nor has the LORD chosen this one. Jesse had seven of his sons pass before Samuel, but Samuel said to him, "The LORD has not chosen these. So he asked Jesse, "Are these*

all the sons you have?
Notice that the first three men were the ones Saul chose to be in his army. He was looking at the physical appearance. Don't let appearance deceive you. There will be several Eliab, Abinadab and Shammah blocking the path of your inheritance, and in David's case, he did not even know about it.

"There is still the youngest," Jesse answered. "He is tending the sheep."

In David's case, they had to look at six people before he was remembered. I don't know what your case is; maybe you were supposed to be the 10th person, but they just saw the 7th, and you have two more people before it gets to your turn.

Two statements defined David: 'The youngest', and 'Tending the sheep'. These two statements alone classify David as an Ant in terms of size, ability and work. What statements have they used to classify you in the past? Somehow you still believe what they called you several years ago; and though you are born again now, the spirits of those names still follow you and torment you.

The Youngest: Tells me he can't achieve anything great. He is either too weak, or not old enough to make things happen.

Tending the Sheep: Means what he is earning cannot be enough, what he is doing is not that important. However, it was from these two classifications that characterize an Ant that God used to elevate David.

He learned from being the youngest how to trust God for his promotion. He learned from tending the sheep how to fight the enemy (the Lion and the Bear). He learned from being the youngest and tending the sheep how to be the greatest musician and psalmist. (Purpose discovered). David never allowed his size or his Job to define him. God is telling you and I that, that which we consider as a barrier or limitation should not be overlooked, and what we consider a barrier can actually be our strength. There is a still small voice in that storm that will propel you from obscurity to limelight.

> **...that which we consider as a barrier or limitation should not be overlooked, and what we consider a barrier can actually be our strength.**

****

In the Cave of Adullam

Psalm 142 - *A prayer of David when he was in the cave.*

Psalm 142 can easily be referred to as the psalm of loneliness. The prayer in this psalm was a different type of loneliness prayer that David prayed. This was a prayer of someone in extreme pain, abandoned by the society. It was a prayer of mercy, fear and abandonment. It was a prayer that demands urgent attention, and a desperate cry for help in time of trouble.

You have to understand that it is easy to feel lonely when

help is taking too long; you can feel lonely when it looks like you are getting out of favor with God, and instead of things getting better, they are actually getting worse. Though David was lonely and felt that everyone was against him, it was the last part of his prayer in Psalm 142 that changed his TEST to TESTIMONY: *"Set me free from my prison that I may praise your name, then the righteous will gather about me, because of your goodness to me".*

In David's TEST, he left room for God in his prayer.

1 Samuel 22:1-5 (NIV)
David left Gath and escaped to the cave of Adullam. When his brothers and his father's household heard about it, they went down to him there. All those who were in distress or in debt or discontented gathered around him, and he became their commander. About four hundred men were with him. From there David went to Mizpah in Moab and said to the king of Moab, "Would you let my father and mother come and stay with you until I learn what God will do for me? So he left them with the king of Moab, and they stayed with him as long as David was in the stronghold. But the prophet Gad said to David, "Do not stay in the stronghold. Go into the land of Judah." So David left and went to the forest of Hereth.

Adullam is a cave in the wilderness; and the wilderness is where nothing stands, nor survives. The cave became a place of refuge, a place where men with pain, men with issues, men with problems, came to reside with David. Adullam means "Justice of the People"

Here we see David's dreams of a fulfilled destiny lay

wrecked before him. He was now fired from his job; fired by Saul, and became a fugitive. From the comfort of the palace, he found himself now fighting for survival in the wilderness. He was at the lowest point of his life alone in the dark cave, sleeping on dirt, no food, no one to talk to, no hope of anything changing. Simply put, David became nothing and had nothing.

He was there at the cave, unable to sleep sometimes, for fear of being killed by wild animals. It was while in the cave, he wrote Psalm 142. What psalm are you writing right now? Does the psalm you are writing give room for God to operate like David did? Or is your psalm full of complaints and bitterness against God?

1 Chronicles 12:22
Day after Day men came to David until he had a great army like the army of God

Who were the people that met David at the cave?
1. **Distressed Men** - Psychological suffering, extreme physical pain, facing severe financial trouble.
2. **Discontented men** - Men dissatisfied with their present situation, or men craving for something more.
3. **In-debt men** - Men sinking financially.

We can have all, or some of the attributes, but whatever your case may be, you can relate to these men that came to David at Adullam. The question is, how do you move from Distress, Discontented, in debt to 'The Mighty Men'. These men were about 400 in number that increased to over 200,000 fighting men. How did they do it? We can trace all these to what happened at Adullam.

What happened at the cave of Adullam?
What transformed these men?
What did David tell them at Adullam?
What did they go through to become what they were?

David taught these men certain principles that transformed them. These principles include:

Improve your skills:
They suddenly found out that they have enough time to think of their situation. They learnt something new on their down time. What are you learning on your down time? We must realize that the way we did things 5 years ago have changed. Things are revolving and evolving. Learn something new.
-The men also looked at something they had never done before, and learnt what to do by taking baby steps.
-Some of these men learnt how to shoot arrows using both hands, left and right hands. Do you know how difficult it is to learn how to use the left hand in old age?

Transference of energy:
They discovered and learnt that when people reject you, you don't get mad at them, but rather you improve yourself. It would have been easier to be mad at the society, angry with God, or be angry with everyone, but rather than be angry, they got better with passion: the energy that would have been spent getting angry, was spent to getting better.

Surviving the process of time:
David's men found a way to survive in the process of time. Are you on your process of time, where your story

will be told someday? David's men did not faint while waiting, they found a way to get stronger while waiting. God is a God of process; the process of time develops strength and character. Joseph went through a process of time after he told his dreams and was sold into slavery, he went through his process of time before he became the Prime Minister.

Know your destination:
They learnt that it is about where they are going, and not where they were coming from.
- You can't change the past, but you can affect the future
- The past has the tendency to slow you down.

Priority:
Ability to know the right priority will determine how far you will go in life. Priority protects your decision, and priority also protects your life.

Rebuild:
At the cave, they started rebuilding the future, it may not be easy, but it was steady and God honored them

Information:
They had new information. In this age and time, information is the key. The news you hear will more often than not, feed you with information that will discourage you. You can look for information that will change your life.
How do you use technology to help you? At Adullam they were separated, blocked from the negative news of depression, frustration and fear.

Determination:
They were determined and became serious; this was not a job for the frivolous, nor the foolish; they were prepared, physically and mentally.

Identity:
They changed the names people called them, and embraced the name God called them. It's time to embrace the name God has called you. Has God called you blessed, then you must be blessed. Has God called you great, then you must be great.
For a long time, Gideon was living up the names that people called him: 'weakest in Manasseh and the least of the whole house of Israel', until God visited him at the threshing floor and called him "thou mighty man of valor".
These men changed their names from 'Distress, Discontented, in-debt' to 'The Mighty Men of David'.

David made room for God in his life struggles, and God came through for him. He told the men these valuable truth that changed their lives at Adullam, whereby they became a strong army to be reckoned with. These men learnt how to be leaders and take responsibility of their destiny.

****

A Single Cluster of Grapes

The single cluster of grapes represents a single idea that God gives you, yet it is so big that the outcome outweighs you or outgrows you.

Numbers 13: 21-25
So they went up and explored the land from the Desert of Zin as far as Rehob, toward Lebo Hamath. They went up through the Negev and came to Hebron, where Ahiman, Sheshai and Talmai, the descendants of Anak, lived. (Hebron had been built seven years before Zoan in Egypt.) When they reached the Valley of Eshkol,[a] they cut off a branch bearing a single cluster of grapes. Two of them carried it on a pole between them, along with some pomegranates and figs. That place was called the Valley of Eshkol because of the cluster of grapes the Israelites cut off there. At the end of forty days they returned from exploring the land.

The valley of Eshkol is a place where the people of God had to decide on what to do. It is that point in your life where you must make a major decision to face your fears or continue running. It is where you face the facts or the truth. Unfortunately, the truth and the fact do not always agree. It is that point when you pray for a long time for God to give you an idea, and you are stuck between the opinion of people and God's opinion.

How do you define a single cluster of grapes? Why were the grapes so big that it took two men to carry this single cluster of grapes? What is the significance of this single cluster of grapes?

Psalm 62:11
God has spoken once, Twice I have heard this: That power belongs to God.

As they explored the land, they saw the following people:
1. Descendants of Anak
2. Amalekites
3. Hittites
4. Jebusites
5. Amorites

These people were enemies, who constantly attacked the Israelites. They were like a thorn in the flesh, but the one that scared them most were the descendants of Anak.

You know, sometimes, you might have some obstacles that you feel you can handle without any help, but at other times there are obstacles that come to you, and you just feel like God has to intervene on this one. The Israelites were not that scared of the Amalekites or all the other 'ites', but the Anaks were their biggest problem, because they were of great stature and courage.

What do you see as a giant in your inheritance? I want you to look at this picture in your mind: A single Cluster of Grapes and Giants in the Land. The children of God were looking at the single Cluster of Grapes, and then remembered the giants in the land. They were going back and forth, thinking and weighing the options: 'A single cluster of grapes; giants in the land'. They could not bring themselves to accept that there could be more from where the single cluster of grapes came from, and anyway, they had to go through the giants first, or even fight them.

However, you see the light at the end of the tunnel, but

between where you are standing and where the light is coming from, is a dark tunnel that is scary, filled with giants and maybe scorpions, and all types of wild animals. Make no mistake about it, every Promise Land has its giants, just like you are a giant to the ants, but it did not stop them from gathering and storing their food, though they stood the risk of being crushed under your foot. Every blessing has its obstacles. Giants in the land represent the following as we step into our inheritance:

1. **Giant of forgetfulness:** They had been delivered by a mighty God, but they forgot too soon. Have you forgotten how you were sick and you prayed to God to heal you and God healed you? Have you forgotten when you were jobless and asked God to give you a job, now God gave you the job, but you are using the job as an excuse. They forgot the song that says, 'count your blessings name them one by one and see what the Lord has done'. If we group the things that God has done for us without naming them one by one, we may forget the everyday blessings, and even some major blessings.

2. **Giant of fear:** If I step into this land, I hope they won't crush me. If I venture into this area, I hope the giants won't step on me like I step on ants. The giant of fear can affect you physically, emotionally, spiritually, and of course, financially. Several Years ago, TD Jakes preached a message on this titled "Grasshoppers don't Eat Grapes"

3. **Giant of commitment:** What you inherit, you must be committed to take care of it. Some of us are afraid of commitment. They never had the spirit of ownership, because they have been slaves for a long time, and this

whole commitment issue was new to them.

Have we been slaves to lack for such a long time that when we see plenty, we don't recognize it? The single cluster of grapes was evidence that they brought to show Moses. The single cluster of grapes is single, yet so big, it took two men to carry it.
The single cluster of grapes represent a single idea that God gives you, yet it is so big that the outcome outweighs you, or outgrows you. The single cluster of grapes represents a single idea, or substance that God gives, and when processed, it is bigger than how it was gotten raw.

God was telling them, the evidence you got from the land, where the Anaks are staying would do the following for you.
1. **Wealth:** You can sell the wine and create wealth to sustain you, from that single cluster of grape

Deuteronomy 8:18
But remember the LORD your God, for it is he who gives you the ability to produce wealth, and so confirms his covenant, which he swore to your forefathers, as it is today.

Laban cheated Jacob for so many years until God gave Jacob an idea on how to get wealth from his master, Laban. The ability to produce wealth, talks about the strength, along with the idea to go the extra mile. The power gives you the push not to remain average, but strive towards greater heights. How many of us need that extra push or ability today? Why would God give us that power? Because He is Almighty and He alone owns the cattle on a thousand hills.

2. **Health:** God can heal supernaturally, no doubt about that; but God also gave the wisdom to doctors to cure some diseases, or do surgeries, etc. So from the single cluster of grapes, you get health.

3. **Idea:** An idea is a concept or mental impression. There are tons of success stories that simply began with an idea that was developed into something very special. What is an idea worth? It depends on what the person that has the idea is willing to do with it.

Perhaps, you have been given the idea some years ago, but you are still looking at the Anaks. It is time go back to that idea and get on the planning table. The days of manna falling from heaven is gone; the only manna you will receive is the single cluster of grapes, which is an idea.

A single cluster of grapes cannot be taken for granted. You may have been carrying that single cluster of grapes for so many years without realizing that this is where your breakthrough lies. You may have been neglecting the grapes for some time now, and God is saying it is time to turn around and see the value of a single cluster of grapes.

****

From the Valley of Eshkol

The Valley of Eshkol was the valley where the Hebrew spies found a cluster of grapes so large that it took two men to carry it (Numbers 13:23-24).

Understand that whatever you eventually achieve in life, you will not achieve by folding your hands.

Numbers 13:1-2
And the Lord said to Moses, Send men to explore and scout out [for yourselves] the land of Canaan, which I give to the Israelites. From each tribe of their fathers you shall send a man, every one a leader or head among them.

God gave Moses the commandment to send men to explore and scout for themselves the land of Canaan. Remember that this was the land of their inheritance, so why will God tell them to still explore what He has given to them? God is simply saying, 'I created the land, I put things in place, I know where the good stuff are located, I know where you will really enjoy this land, but I am not going to tell you, unless you take the initiative upon yourself to explore what I have given to you for yourself'.

To Explore means, to travel in or go through (an unfamiliar country or area) in order to learn about, or familiarize oneself with it.

It was not Moses that told the people; it was God that told them to do so. God has seen the land, but the people had not seen the land; so He wanted them to explore for themselves, for the following reasons:

Responsibility: He wanted them to be reliable, to be responsible. Statistics shows that 95% of people who win the lottery are broke in three years. These people did not work for this money (don't get me wrong 5% of them are still rich, because they invested wisely); but when you are not responsible for something you mishandle it. *"Responsibility is the price of greatness"*- Winston Churchill. If you want to be great, you must be responsible.

Excitement Level: Excitement is a feeling of great enthusiasm and eagerness. If we don't get excited about our own dream, we may not get to the level God wants us to get to. So our excitement level will be raised when we begin to see the possibilities, as we explore the land. There were specific people that God wanted Moses to send, each one a leader, or a head among them. God is interested in leaders, He wanted the leaders to broaden their knowledge, He wanted them to be able to make good judgment based on what they saw in Canaan. In raising their excitement level, He wanted them to see HOW GOOD the land was. The land was flowing with milk and honey; it was a good inheritance. He wanted them to compare the land from where they were coming from, and also with what they have passed through.

Trust Level: Has your trust level been downgraded as you explored? Was there a time when you just doubted God? May be not openly, but in your heart. God wanted to see what level of Trust they will have if they explore the land.

Choice: How you trust will determine what you choose. In other words, trust and choice are members of the same family. The Valley of Eshkol is the valley of decision, where we have to weigh our options in other to decide if we really want to step into the land of our inheritance. Our lives are the sum total of the decisions we have made.

Numbers 13:17-20
When Moses sent them to explore Canaan, he said, "Go up through the Negev and on into the hill country. See what the land is like and whether the people who live there are strong or weak, few or many. What kind of land do they live in? Is it good or bad? What kind of towns do they live in? Are they unwalled or fortified? How is the soil? Is it fertile or poor? Are there trees in it or not? Do your best to bring back some of the fruit of the land." (It was the season for the first ripe grapes.)

NOW This is what a leader does: God told Moses, a leader, to select leaders to explore the land. I tried to break down the reasons why God wanted to use leaders, as well as why He wanted them to explore the land. Moses went beyond that through prayers, and told them the following:

See if the people are strong or Weak: Know your enemy. If you don't know the strength of your enemy, you may have lost the battle before even starting. To see how to defeat the system is to check for loopholes. There are strategies you need to know to fight effectively, you need to know your enemy's strengths and weaknesses. God will tell you how to go to a battle based on your assessment.

When David came to bring food for his brothers at the battle field, he saw an enemy that was strong, he assessed the enemy as a giant with all the battle equipment, but David was not only looking at him physically, as he was speaking, he was also assessing him spiritually. The first thing he saw was that he was an uncircumcised Philistine, so he was not in the covenant. The second thing David saw, as he assessed the giant, was that he was able to know exactly where to hit with the stone for maximum impact. You have to know where the strongholds are. A stronghold is a place that has been fortified so as to protect it against attack.

Some jobs you are applying for have been fortified, some businesses you are trying to get into have been fortified, and some positions you are considering have been fortified. If we know where the strongholds are, we need wisdom and direction from God on how to attack.

Few or Many: Few or many go beyond occupancy or square footage. Few or many tell you if there are opportunities in that area of your career. Few or many tell you if there's a demand on what you want to do this year. God has to open your eyes to see the spiritual few or many, because the news can tell you something, and God can say that is not the case.

What type of land they live in: If the land is good or bad for them. What works for one may not work for another.

What type of Towns: what is significant in this town? What is the mode of worship here: Christian, Islam, idol, etc.

Are they walled or fortified: Understanding of the security system and how it works is very crucial to your entrance, or occupation of that land.

6. **How is the soil:** Is it fertile soil, good for planting, or is it poor. They were mostly farmers, shepherds, so they need to know if they will be able to sustain their families.

7. **Are there trees in it or not:** If there are no trees, then its more of a desert and may not be habitable.

8. **Do your best to bring back some of the fruits of the land:** bring back evidence to show that you really went to the land

Chapter Three

The Makeover

"When I was a child, I thought like a child, I reasoned like a child. When I became a man, I put childish ways behind me"
1 Corinthians 13:11

All the troubling 'what ifs' in the world did in fact align themselves against the hapless Saul, as they went round and round the same mountain, day after day, searching for the fleeing woman, and hoping for a different outcome. He eventually gave up, and went to the town of Carmel to set up a monument to himself, before heading home, while Samuel went looking for him. When the aging Prophet finally found him, Saul greeted him cheerfully. "May the Lord bless you," he said. "I have carried out the Lord's command!" Samuel fixed a baleful, tear-stained face upon Saul. The tears that ran down the Prophet's face confused Saul; spreading out his palms, and shoulders raised, he said with a wide grin, "I carried out God's command concerning the Amalekites"

Samuel stood in silence, obviously wincing, while his joints straightened. He pointed a bony finger in the direction from which Saul entered. "Why then are my ears suddenly full of the bleating of sheep and the lowing of oxen".

Saul could feel the blood drain from his face. He had hoped to placate the old man with news of their overwhelming victory. After all, what was a 'slight deviation' (a surviving king, a few expendable wives, and some spoils for sacrifice), compared to the extermination of an entire nation? Anyone should be happy with that.
Samuel shook his head, his rage clearly growing by the moment. "You have rejected the Word of the Lord, and the Lord has rejected you as king over Israel"

Einstein's definition of insanity is "doing the same thing over and over, and expecting a different result". If you are doing the same things over and over again, and expecting different results, it is time for you to get a spiritual makeover, so that you don't truncate your own destiny. Saul had disobeyed and carried on the same attitude one time too many; he was long overdue for a makeover, but never realized he actually needed one desperately.

A makeover is a complete reconstruction and renovation of something; a change of heart and attitude; learning to walk in total obedience; shedding off carelessness; adopting a new strategy to living. At some point in life, a makeover becomes necessary, in order for us to thrive as Christians. Let us go deeper on why we do need a makeover:

We need a spiritual makeover, because God expects us to outgrow certain things. Hence, the way you did things two years ago will not be the way you will do things tomorrow or next. The statement, "as it was in the beginning so shall it be", has to do with the Almighty God, the Creator of the universe. It does not apply to us in the context of us getting better, having a different approach to the things that affect us daily.

1 Corinthians 13:11
"When I was a child, I thought like a child, I reasoned like a child. When I became a man, I put childish ways behind me"

The makeover enables us to see things differently, so that what gets you angry before will no longer get you angry, what irritates you easily, will no longer be the case. The makeover helps you value the position that God has placed you in. The makeover enables you to have a new way of processing and accessing things.

We need a spiritual makeover, because the devil is not relaxing on his plans to kill, steal and destroy. We need that makeover to be able to withstand all the wiles of the enemy; to block loopholes, by uploading spiritual patch, like software updates, antivirus updates that captures new viruses. The make over enables us to capture new tricks of the devil.

Ephesians 6:10-11
In conclusion, be strong in the Lord [be empowered through your union with Him]; draw your strength from Him [that strength which His boundless might provides]. Put on God's whole armor [the armor of a heavy-armed soldier which God supplies], that you may be able successfully to stand up against [all] the strategies and the deceits of the devil.

As the days progress, the strategies and deceits of the enemy will be on a higher level, so we need to put on the whole armor, not some of the armor. It is not being a Christian on Sunday, and being something else on Monday. It is very important to stay armed always, because: *"we are not wrestling with flesh and blood [contending only with physical opponents], but against the despotisms, against the powers, against [the master spirits who are] the world rulers of this present darkness, against the spirit forces of wickedness in the heavenly (supernatural) sphere".* Ephesians 6:12

I do not need to tell any one of us what is going on in the nation, how people no longer value lives; these troubles are not ordinary, we are contending against the master spirits.

Ephesians 6:13
Therefore put on God's complete armor, that you may be able to resist and stand your ground on the evil day [of danger], and, having done all [the crisis demands], to stand [firmly in your place].

Notice that it says 'Gods complete armor'. Is it possible that we might be operating with incomplete armor? Yes! Is it possible that we might be operating with somebody's armor, like David tried to do when he wanted to fight the giant? Yes! David told Saul, I have not tried these armor before, so let me use the one I know how to use; the one that I have tried before when I was faced with a lion and a bear.

Ephesians 6:14
Stand therefore [hold your ground], having tightened the belt

of truth around your loins and having put on the breastplate of integrity and of moral rectitude and right standing with God...

Part of the makeover is tightening the belt that may have become loose over the years, through carelessness; through what we have allowed to replace our mindset, or through what we see in the society.

Ephesians 6:15-16 (NLT)
For shoes, put on the peace that comes from the Good News so that you will be fully prepared. In addition to all of these, hold up the shield of faith to stop the fiery arrows of the devil

No one goes to the battle without a shield. Don't loose your shield, and if your shield has been battered due to the several battles you have had to fight, then there is need for a makeover.

Ephesians 6:17
And take the helmet of salvation and the sword that the Spirit wields, which is the Word of God.

This is what we are trying to do now, activating the Word of God, standing on His promises, declaring His Word.

Ephesians 6:18
Pray at all times (on every occasion, in every season) in the Spirit, with all [manner of] prayer and entreaty. To that end keep alert and watch with strong purpose and perseverance, interceding in behalf of all the saints (God's consecrated people).

We need a makeover because God wants to start something new with us, and what we are right now cannot handle the new.

Mark 2:22
And no one puts new wine into old wineskin; if he does, the wine will burst the skins, and the wine is lost and the bottles destroyed; but new wine is to be put in new (fresh) wineskin.

New wine represents new levels that we are to step into. New wine also represents new responsibilities, and new positions.

Jeremiah 18:1
This is the word that came to Jeremiah from the Lord: Go down to the potter's house, and there I will give you my message.

I meditated on this for some time, why didn't God just give His message to brother Jerry where he was standing? I came to the following conclusions:
- God wanted Jerry not to be distracted with what was going on.
- Jerry has seen so much happen, and there is a possibility that he may have began to act and think like the people; as the saying goes, "birds of the same feather flock together", but someone said, "birds that flock together will eventually develop the same feathers".

God is simply saying, leave what your gossip buddies told you on how to train your children; how to run your home; how to date; how to behave; go down to the potters house, I have a new message for you. You can't han-

dle the message where you are standing; you may never comprehend the urgency of this message if I just give it to you where you are right now.
The next question was why the Potters house? Why not a synagogue, see a Rabbi? Why the Potters house?

Jeremiah 18:3-10
So I went down to the potter's house, and I saw him working at the wheel. But the pot he was shaping from the clay was marred in his hands; so the potter formed it into another pot, shaping it as seemed best to him. Then the word of the Lord came to me. He said, "Can I not do with you, Israel, as this potter does?" declares the Lord. "Like clay in the hand of the potter, so are you in my hand, Israel. If at any time I announce that a nation or kingdom is to be uprooted, torn down and destroyed, and if that nation I warned repents of its evil, then I will relent and not inflict on it the disaster I had planned. And if at another time I announce that a nation or kingdom is to be built up and planted, and if it does evil in my sight and does not obey me, then I will reconsider the good I had intended to do for it.

The makeover is a spiritual reconstruction that puts us on the same page with what God wants us to become. God is depending heavily on us to stand our grounds, to use the whole armor, instead of some armor.

Isaiah 6:1-9
In the year that King Uzziah died, I saw the Lord seated on a throne, high and exalted, and the train of his robe filled the temple. Above him were seraphs, each with six wings: With two wings they covered their faces, with two they covered their feet, and with two they were flying. And they were call-

ing to one another: "Holy, holy, holy is the LORD Almighty; the whole earth is full of his glory." At the sound of their voices the doorposts and thresholds shook and the temple was filled with smoke. "Woe to me!" I cried. "I am ruined! For I am a man of unclean lips, and I live among a people of unclean lips, and my eyes have seen the King, the LORD Almighty." Then one of the seraphs flew to me with a live coal in his hand, which he had taken with tongs from the altar. With it he touched my mouth and said, "See, this has touched your lips; your guilt is taken away and your sin atoned for." Then I heard the voice of the Lord saying, "Whom shall I send? And who will go for us?" And I said, "Here am I. Send me!" He said, "Go and tell this people:"

From the above Scripture, it is clear that before Isaiah could be commissioned he needed a makeover. It was not much of a problem for Isaiah to see the Lord, or know of what God wants of him, because he saw the Lord. It was the singing of the angels that shook the temple, because God was entering the temple. The bible says that smoke filled the temple, no wonder the doorpost and threshold shook. The Potter had entered the house to do His work on the clay, Isaiah. Between that period, Isaiah had gone through all the steps that was mentioned about the clay and the Potter.

...when God wants to use you for a higher calling, you will need a makeover...

After the Potter finished His work, Isaiah suddenly came to the realization 'that he was a man of unclean lips, and he dwells among the people of unclean lips'. (Understand that before now, Isaiah did not realize that this was a problem; it was not an issue for him). 'Isaiah was able to answer the call after the Potter worked on him'.

This is the same reason you see some Christians, though they have accepted Jesus, they speak in tongues, but they live in the midst of all things wrong, and are not even bothered by it. However, a time will come when God wants to use you for a higher calling, you will need a makeover; and after you get the makeover, you will begin to discover that some things you thought were not an issue, is really an issue, and you will need to deal with it. There is a higher calling for you. Be ready for a Makeover!

****

Connecting with Destiny

"The only person you are destined to become is the person you decide to be" -Ralph Waldo Emerson

God already made a decision about you before he made the world, before you were born. He gave us dominion and gave us inheritance before He said, "Let there be Light", as is seen in this verse:

Romans 8:29
God knew them before he made the world. And he decided that they would be like His Son. Then Jesus would be the firstborn of many brothers and sisters.

Deuteronomy 30:19
Today I am giving you a choice of two ways. And I ask heav-

en and earth to be witnesses of your choice. You can choose life or death. The first choice will bring a blessing. The other choice will bring a curse. So choose life! Then you and your children will live.

The second verse tells us that in as much as God has given you the world, you still have to make a choice, if you really want it or not. You have a choice to succeed or fail, to be richly blessed in the world or not. God says the choice is yours to make.

> **We are a sum total of all the choices we have made since we were born.**

We see mankind constantly on the crossroad between good and evil. We are a sum total of all the choices we have made since we were born. Saul made a choice to keep what God says to destroy completely, and we all know the outcome of that choice.

As someone who wants to be where God wants you to be, or who wants to be doing what you have been destined to do, you must, once in a while, try to ask some specific questions to your maker.
1. Why were you born?
2. What were the specific reasons why you were made?
3. Am I doing what I was made to do, or am I on the wrong path?
4. The choices or decisions I'm about to make in life, how does that help my destiny?

Most people do what they do because that was what they saw people doing, or because that was what they were told to do. Some will go to any length to discover their purpose, while some don't really care, as long as they are able to get by, they are fine. Thus, there are so many get-by people, who stand on the road network of destiny trying to catch a ride to any where, not caring if its supposed to be their destination or not.

As I think on this, two words come to mind "Connect and Destiny"

Connect means to bring together, or into contact, so that a real or notional link is established. It also means to join together, so as to provide access and communication. Therefore, you connect when there's no communication, and you connect when you have no idea what is going on.

Destiny is the events that will necessarily happen to a particular person or thing in the future. It is the hidden power believed to control what will happen in the future.

However, I will define destiny as the destination of a person or people, who already had a pre-knowledge of where they are going, and determined that they will get there.

The key words being:
- The event that will necessarily happen to a particular person
- Knowing where you are going and making up your mind to get there.

In other words, connecting with Destiny will mean bringing together the links to events that will necessarily happen to you. So, could it be that there are times that we should make conscious effort to connect when we sense that there is a disconnect somewhere? – Emphatically yes. Would there be times that you will have to go through some specific events, which you have no control over? Yes

> **For us to get to our destination we must trust the One who created the road, as well as the road map**

"Destiny is not a matter of chance; it is a matter of choice. It is not a thing to be waited for, it is a thing to be achieved." — William Jennings Bryan

Based on these facts, we see that we can alter our destiny; we can make it better, and we can stay on course, which is the original purpose God created us. We have the will and the Power to decide our destiny; but I also discovered that God, being who He is, could pull you out of your comfort zone to connect you to your destiny. It may not be business as usual, and it may be uncomfortable. You may have to go through a certain process to achieve greatness, and connect with destiny.

Another significant factor in connecting with Destiny is TRUST.
For us to get to our destination we must trust the One who created the road, as well as the road map. Trust in the Lord, not with half your heart, but with all your heart and lean not on your own understanding. A lot of us think that since we can afford a physical map of life, or a GPS of life, do the right thing, stay healthy, be careful, etc., that we will be fine. Some of us try to play smart with God, and He is just there looking at us, and shaking

His head. We have come to trust our instincts, we have trusted man, we have trusted our bosses or jobs, we have trusted some predictions, but we have not trusted God to connect us to our destiny.

Two of Jesus disciples were on the wrong path to their destination, or destiny.
He said to one, Judas, ***"You are about to betray the Son of God, that which you want to do, do it quickly"***. He said to another one, Peter, ***'Satan has decided to sift you as wheat, but I have prayed for you"***.

So what did both of them do that made a difference?
This was what Peter did:
- Peter decided to trust God to reconnect back to his destiny.
- Peter decided to confront that which made him deny Jesus.
- Peter decided to be bold and talk about Jesus anywhere; he did what he had to do to reconnect back to his destiny. Peter got an absolute makeover.

This was what Judas did:
- Judas felt he could no longer reconnect back to God because of the grievous sin he committed
- He was not ready to confront the issue at stake.
- Judas couldn't live with himself, so he took his own life to end it all, which is not a solution at all.

****

Laban's Goats: It's all about the Vision

"That night all the members of the community raised their voices and wept aloud" Numbers 14:1

Laban's goats were not really Laban's, but Israel's goats. Goats in this sense represent our inheritance; it refers to what God has promised us. It's all about what you see, how you see, and when you see.

Vision can be defined as the capacity to see farther than your eyes can see. It is having an awareness of something *(this is beyond the surface)*, and an action *(what do you do with what you are aware of)*. Your awareness will determine your attitude, which will eventually affect your actions. Vision can be better understood from the following scripture:

Numbers 14:1-12
That night all the members of the community raised their voices and wept aloud. All the Israelites grumbled against Moses and Aaron, and the whole assembly said to them, "If only we had died in Egypt! Or in this wilderness! Why is the LORD bringing us to this land only to let us fall by the sword? Our wives and children will be taken as plunder. Wouldn't it be better for us to go back to Egypt?" And they said to each other, "We should choose a leader and go back to Egypt. Then Moses and Aaron fell facedown in front of the whole Israelite assembly gathered there. Joshua son of Nun and Caleb son of Jephunneh, who were among those who had explored the land, tore their clothes, and said to the entire Israelite assembly, "The land we passed through and explored is exceedingly good. If the LORD is pleased with us, he will

lead us into that land, a land flowing with milk and honey, and will give it to us. Only do not rebel against the LORD. And do not be afraid of the people of the land, because we will devour them. Their protection is gone, but the LORD is with us. Do not be afraid of them. But the whole assembly talked about stoning them. Then the glory of the LORD appeared at the tent of meeting to all the Israelites. The LORD said to Moses, "How long will these people treat me with contempt? How long will they refuse to believe in me, in spite of all the signs I have performed among them? I will strike them down with a plague and destroy them, but I will make you into a nation greater and stronger than they.

They saw the land, they were aware of what was going on; it obviously affected their attitude, going by their response: they wept aloud and complained bitterly, they even thought of stoning Caleb and Joshua. Here, we see a people who were defined by what they saw.

What you see can affect you positively or negatively. It depends on how you interpret it.

What you see can affect you positively or negatively. It depends on how you interpret it. They saw the single cluster of grapes, and they saw the giants too. What they saw immediately gave them a feeling or perception of the future. They sealed their destiny with their own words, as a result of their perception. You must be careful with your words, some of us need a total makeover with our words. What you say should not be taken for granted. They confessed that it was better for them to die in the wilderness than to enter their inheritance. There is a tendency for things to seem to get worse after a prolonged praying and fasting. The kingdom of darkness has been shaken, and so they are fighting harder, because they have been injured. It's only a matter of time before you see a seriously wounded lion finally slow down and die. So it's not out of place that things will be rough a little bit.

On this fateful Tuesday, I went to Church not feeling too good, and a little angry about some things, including the heating system that suddenly packed up, but then as I prepared the message for the mid-week service, I realized what Caleb said.

Numbers 14:9
Only do not rebel against the LORD. And do not be afraid of the people of the land, because we will devour them. Their protection is gone, but the LORD is with us. Do not be afraid of them.

I tell you today, their protection is gone, but the Lord is with you.

Proverbs 29:18
Where there is no revelation, the people cast off restraint; but blessed is he who keeps the law.

VISION IS ACTION!
- Do we have the courage to do what we see?
- Do we have the courage to go ahead with that plan or proposal?
- Do we have the courage to declare what God showed us, or asked us to do?

It is not enough to pray for one month, and after that relax. It is not enough to say, "I believe God will sort me out", and after that you wait and do nothing. God needs something to work with from you; something tangible, something He can hold on to. What have you added to your prayers?

After Laban agreed to Jacob's proposal, Laban hid all the spotted goats, and sent Jacob so far away that it will take three days journey for Jacob to get to him, just in case he decides to come back to steal the spotted goats at night. He made it almost impossible for Jacob, but Jacob used the power of vision to get what he wanted.

Genesis 30:37-43
Then Jacob cut green branches from poplar and almond trees. He stripped off some of the bark so that the branches had white stripes on them. He put the branches in front of the flocks at the watering places. When the animals came to drink, they also mated in that place. Then when the goats mated in front of the branches, the young that were born were spotted, striped, or black. Jacob separated the spotted and the black animals from the other animals in the flock. He kept his animals separate from Laban's. Any time the stronger animals in the flock were mating, Jacob put the branches before their eyes. The animals mated near those branches. But when the weaker animals mated, Jacob did not put the branches there. So the young animals born from the weak animals were Laban's. And the young animals born from the stronger animals were Jacob's. In this way Jacob became very rich. He had large flocks, many servants, camels, and donkeys.

Jacob made sure that the goats were seeing the stripes,

and spotted each time they come to drink water. The goats began to retain stripes in their memory each time they drink water. The only thing they were seeing were stripes; hence, the only thing they can produce is stripes. What they saw everyday began to affect their genes, it began to affect their reproductive organs, and so when they produced, they produced stripes and spotted goats. We must see what we want. Do you see yourself getting healed? Do you see yourself running after children or giving birth? Do you see yourself on that dream job? Do you see your children as godly children? Do you see your marriage as a godly marriage? If it can happen to goats that do not have souls, then it is even better for you.

As soon as he knew what he wanted, Jacob looked for what, or how this can be achieved. He stepped out of his comfort zone, he didn't wait to see if the first goats that mated would produce stripes; he was not praying everyday for God to intervene, and saying, "Father you have heard, let it be so", and then go back to sleep under the shade; no, he acted and God blessed his action. Do you know how many trees that Jacob had to peel their backs before he saw the one that can produce the kind of spots that he wanted? I can assure you that it was not the first tree he cut down. To cut down the trees or branches require some type of effort; it also requires some time. What time are you creating to achieve what you want? After the first, second, or third tree that he cut down, discouragement must have set in, but he continued to look at other branches, until he saw what he wanted.

What was supposed to occur naturally was changed

by what Jacob saw. What you see will eventually affect what you get.

Chapter Four

Unrestricted Access

"High expectations are the key to everything" –Sam Walton

Judith, in excruciating pain, limped back to her Caravan, swallowed her painkillers with an icy drink, and then crawled into her hard bed. She slept soundly until 4 in the afternoon, woken only by her British roommate, Beverly singing, 'Glory to God in the highest'. Judith sat up, suddenly discovering every bone in her body was shouting out complaints; she could hardly move.
Beverly looked at her with glee, "You will get stronger", she said.
"No, it's been three years, and the pain only gets worse. No, I will never get better, let alone stronger, I hate my life", Judith declared sadly.
"That is a negative attitude Judith; you must be positive and hopeful; be expectant of better days ahead, that's the only way to win this battle…"

It is important that the battle must be won first on the inside before we begin to see the manifestation on the outside; you must learn to be expectant.

Proverbs 10:28 (ESV)
The hope of the righteous brings joy, but the expectation of the wicked will perish.

Proverbs 23:18 (ESV)
Surely there is a future, and your hope will not be cut off.

If the Lord is talking about a 'future', surely things must have been put in place, but we must 'hope' for it. The Key word is 'hope', which is a feeling of expectation and desire for certain things to happen. The first thing we need to get access to this packaged future is a relationship. This is a connection, an association or involvement.

Mathew 15:25-26
The woman came and knelt before him. "Lord, help me!" she said. He replied, it is not right to take the children's bread and toss it to their dogs.

This scripture is talking about the faith of a woman who actually got what she wanted; but take a deep look at this story one more time:
- Jesus was telling the woman that those whom He has a relationship with, He cannot deny them.
- He was also saying that those whom He is associated with or connected to, already have bread made especially for them; hence, it is their inheritance.

Also, the relationship has to grow, or be developed with holiness. In other words, the depth of our relationship with God is directly proportional to the state of our holiness. God has a nature; His nature is holiness. To have access, you must have the key, and not just any key, but the key of David.

Isaiah 22:22
I will place on his shoulder the key to the house of David; what he opens no one can shut, and what he shuts no one can open.

Revelation 3:7
[To the Church in Philadelphia] To the angel of the church in Philadelphia write: These are the words of him who is holy and true, who holds the key of David. What he opens no one can shut, and what he shuts no one can open.

The key of David can only be received by a special group of people who have the understanding that David had, and has the knowledge that David had. This key can only be received through a personal relationship with God. Up until now, we have some type of access. We have had access to some things, but some things are still shielded from us, due to lack of relationship.

1Chronicles 4:9-10
Jabez was more honorable than his brothers. His mother had named him Jabez, saying, "I gave birth to him in pain." Jabez cried out to the God of Israel, "Oh, that you would bless me and enlarge my territory! Let your hand be with me, and keep me from harm so that I will be free from pain." And God granted his request.

The book of 1Chronicles was not really about Jabez, it was generally talking about the descendants of Judah, and Jabez happens to be one of the descendants of Judah. However, something about this fellow, Jabez had to interrupt the writer to focus on him; Jabez did something that caused that interruption:

Verse 9, shows us that Jabez was well respected in the community. For you to be honorable you must be wealthy. Before now, I thought that he prayed that prayer because he was poor and people made fun of him, but no, honorable people are often respected; and they sit in high places.

Furthermore, if you are honorable, you make decisions that affect others, so Jabez must have made decisions that affected his family, as well as his community. Honorable people are people of influence, which means Jabez was a man of influence. Thus, Jabez had some level of access that made him honorable, that made him worthy; but one day, Jabez considered that he should be able to do more than what he is doing now, and decided he cannot settle for just any access, but needs UNRESTRICTED ACCESS. Right there, his search began, and he traced his inability to receive unrestricted access to a generational problem – HIS NAME.

As a believer, you must understand that though you may be doing well, there are some things that you just cannot achieve until you deal with certain limitations in your life. Make some changes, be expectant, and make that expectation quite high.

****

A Taste of Two Cities

"Everyone will have an opportunity, or several opportunities to taste these two cities in some area of their life".

Let's take a look at two scenarios that greatly affect our access in terms of where we are right now, and where we hope to be. Everyone will have an opportunity or several opportunities to taste these two cities in some areas of their lives. These two cities cut across all areas of life: career, business, family, health, wealth, relationships, etc. The thing about taste is the feeling that it leaves on your tongue. Taste can either be bitter or sweet, and sometimes both.

According to Thomas Jefferson, *"Taste cannot be controlled by Law"*. In other words, it comes with its own flavor based on what is bringing the taste. In this day and age where law controls almost everything, Thomas Jefferson's statement still holds true that one thing that cannot be controlled by law is taste.

Nevertheless, God uses illustrations and events to either tell us the state of man, or point us to where we should be going. In the contest of this book, a city will be what you are able to access based on where you are, and you ask yourself:
- Do I have the freedom to do what I love to do?
- Do I have the freedom to live the way I really want to live: health, wealth, spiritually, etc.?

The answers to these questions will determine what city you are living in right now.

The two cities we want to look at are Samaria and Jericho. You are either tasting Samaria right now, or tasting Jericho; or probably even tasting both Samaria and Jericho at the same time. These two cities changed the course of God's children in terms of their inheritance and unrestricted access. These two cities laid down the blueprints of what to do when you find yourself going against the current of life, or the tide of life.

Samaria:

1 Kings 13:32
For the message he declared by the word of the Lord against the altar in Bethel and against all the shrines on the high places in the towns of Samaria will certainly come true.

This is in reference to the prophecy against the altars in Samaria and the old prophet who deceived the man of God to eat where God asked him not to eat. Hence, it is possible to have restricted access in places God has given to you as your inheritance: What have you prophesied concerning your Samaria? The prophet by divine revelation said, whatever was declared will come to pass. Whatever you have said concerning where you are right now, which is known as your Samaria will come true.

Altars were pulled down in Samaria. Progress was everywhere in Samaria. I want to believe that there were songs in Samaria called 'Samaria the beautiful', like we have songs about America the beautiful. I want to believe that Samaria became a land of opportunities, where dreams come true, the land of the free, and home of the brave, Samaria, oh Samaria.

However, suddenly, the peace that Samaria was having becomes threatened. The solid foundations were now shaken; the Samaria cruise ship started having problems, Samaria needs help. Samaria is beginning to look like Egypt when they were in slavery. Samaria is beginning to have a bad taste, because of several reasons, and one major reason being LEADERSHIP. Is something threatening your peace of mind?

1Kings 16:29-34
Now Ahab the son of Omri became king over Israel in the thirty-eighth year of Asa king of Judah, and Ahab the son of Omri reigned over Israel in Samaria twenty-two years. Ahab the son of Omri did evil in the sight of the LORD more than all who were before him. It came about, as though it had been a trivial thing for him to walk in the sins of Jeroboam the son of Nebat, that he married Jezebel the daughter of Ethbaal king of the Sidonians, and went to serve Baal and worshiped him. So he erected an altar for Baal in the house of Baal which he built in Samaria. Ahab also made the Asherah. Thus Ahab did more to provoke the LORD God of Israel than all the kings of Israel who were before him. In his days Hiel the Bethelite built Jericho; he laid its foundations with the loss of Abiram his firstborn, and set up its gates with the loss of his youngest son Segub, according to the word of the LORD, which He spoke by Joshua the son of Nun.

Samaria had leadership problems, this was not the only problem, but it gave birth to all other problems. We see a situation where God cleaned the land for the sake of His people. We see a situation where things were going on well for the people of God. All of a sudden Samaria got a new leader, who reversed everything that was done over the years in Samaria, and Samaria became like Egypt after the death of Joseph.

When Joseph was the Prime Minister, he helped his people in Egypt, established them with vineyards, farms, cattle, etc., until after the king and Joseph died, and the bible says there arose a king that knew not Joseph. Is there a new king in your Samaria that knew not Joseph? Is there an issue that looks like it is resisting what was declared where you are right now? Ahab, for 22 years, reversed what the Samarians enjoyed; their inheritance was taken away from them, and they suffered as a result of the high places that Ahab built in the city of Samaria.

You begin to have the bad taste of Samaria when unpleasant people become your boss, or become your leaders:

Proverbs 29:2 (AMP)
When the [uncompromisingly] righteous are in authority, the people rejoice; but when the wicked man rules, the people groan and sigh.

You begin to experience restricted access to divine health. You begin to have restricted access to happiness; the joy of the Lord is no longer your strength, because FEAR of the unknown has taken over.

1 Kings 18:2
So Elijah went to present himself to Ahab. Now the famine was severe in Samaria...

Samaria was under a siege; external forces were attacking them. These forces caused them not to go out, and nobody could come in. These forces became unbearable to the Samarians. Samaria was constantly under attack, from one battle to another. Do you feel you are constantly fighting battles springing up from left, right, and center? You are in Samaria right now.

2 kings 7:1
Elisha replied, "Hear the word of the LORD. This is what the LORD says: About this time tomorrow, a seah of the finest flour will sell for a shekel and two seahs of barley for a shekel at the gate of Samaria

Are there Elishas that want to pray an *'About this time tomorrow'* kind of prayer? You need this kind of prayer.

Hebrew 4:12
For the word of God is quick, and powerful, and sharper than any two-edged sword, piercing even to the dividing asunder of soul and spirit, and of the joints and marrow, and is a discerner of the thoughts and intents of the heart.

2 kings 7:3
Now there were four men with leprosy at the entrance of the city gate. They said to each other, "Why stay here until we die?

The four men that had leprosy represents what you and I go through when we find ourselves in a place that was once pleasant, a place that was once great, with no problems, until something went wrong. Once upon a time in the lives of these four men, they were free to do whatever they wanted; they were free to go wherever they wanted. The four men had unrestricted access, until leprosy came. Leprosy became a limitation. These four men were already suffering from the siege, and now leprosy. It's like adding salt to injury. We may not have leprosy, but are limited in some areas of our lives. As leprosy came to them, it took away their self-confidence. Have the people you depended on taken away your confidence? Do you have a feeling of discouragement when someone you trusted lied to you?

It was very significant to use these four men. They said to each other, "Why stay here until we die?" They sat down and thought about their situation. They were banished from the land, because of their sickness, but that didn't mean their lives were over. The four men were willing to fight. Your willingness to fight will determine the direction of the battle.

The four men were willing to fight. Your willingness to fight will determine the direction of the battle.

The four men asked themselves questions, "Why stay here until we die?" It was a wake up question for them, and it was the most important question of their life. Sometimes we need to ask ourselves the wake up question. Some questions have been going through your mind about some issues that are affecting you. It's a wake up question! Wake up questions build a kind of strength within you.
- Why do I need to be doing what I'm doing, when I know I can do better, if I change my mindset?
- Why do I keep eating leftovers when I can get fresh

food?
- Why do I keep wishing that some day things would change, when I know within me that things will not change, but I need to change?
Change will confuse your problems... so make that needed change.

"Why Stay here until we die" – Tells us that we have options like these men. You may ask me, are there not people who considered the 'what ifs', and died, lost all they had? Yes, but what if it turned around best for them?

It is time to do something about Samaria. It is time to make that decision that you have been trying to put off, and waiting for God to speak clearly. God is saying you don't need any more confirmation. Before these men were presented with their options on what to do, something had already gone out which was "The Word".

The Word became life. The word will become what you want it to be. It can be superior fire, if you need to burn some things in your life. The Word can be a hammer, if you need to break off from some things. The Word can be a chisel, if you need to chisel out something that is proving difficult to get out of. The Word can chisel you out of a bad habit. The Word can be like a battalion of army that the Syrians heard and they fled. If you need some things to run away from you, the Word can frighten them and off they go.

Most importantly, after the Word, you must make the right move: Step out

****

Jericho: The City of Palm Trees

"While Samaria may be your present situation, Jericho is the future".

The second city to consider is Jericho: The city of Palm Trees. The Palm tree begins to bear fruit after it has been planted for eight years, and continues to be productive for a century. The palm is a beautiful and most useful tree.
-Its fruit is daily food.
-Its sap is used for wine.
-The fibers of the base of its leaves are woven into ropes and rigging.
-Its tall stem supplies a valuable timber.
-Its leaves are made into mats, brushes, and baskets.

Jericho's Arabic name, means "fragrant"; sweet smelling savor. Jericho is a land of promise, which God swore to His children and to their seed. We see Moses, a prophet of God, whom God used to deliver His children; the only human that saw God's back; Moses, who communes with God, and after 40 days, he comes out of the meeting with God, and because he has been in His presence, the reflection from His presence made his face to glow and shine, so much that he had to put a veil to cover his face. This same Moses did not enter the promise land; he was shown the city of palm trees in a place called Pisgah. His access became restricted to Pisgah because he cut short his future by anger.

Analysis of Pisgah
Pisgah in Hebrew refers to a "high place" like the top of

a mountain; but Pisgah to Moses was "See all the things you can get, but you will not touch it." Are there some of us standing at Pisgah right now, looking at the city of palm trees? Our dreams can either die at Pisgah or be reactivated at Pisgah. Pisgah, where Moses caught a glimpse of the city of palm trees, and died, became a motivator to the other people. Pisgah can play two roles: Either for your dreams to die there, or for you to be motivated by what you see from there.

Secondly, it is possible for us to be standing at Pisgah for a very long time analyzing what we have seen, until we over-analyze it, and lose sight of what is important. Some people have met us at Pisgah, seen the same things we saw, and ran with the vision of what they saw.

Deuteronomy 1: 6-8
The Lord our God said to us at Horeb, "You have stayed long enough at this mountain. Break camp and advance into the hill country of the Amorites; go to all the neighboring peoples in the Arabah, in the mountains, in the western foothills, in the Negev and along the coast, to the land of the Canaanites and to Lebanon, as far as the great river, the Euphrates. See, I have given you this land. Go in and take possession of the land the Lord swore he would give to your fathers—to Abraham, Isaac and Jacob—and to their descendants after them.

Some of us have stayed long enough at the mountain called Pisgah. God told them you have analyzed enough; it is time to move on. Over analyzing spiritual things introduces the loopholes of doubt.
It is interesting when you are standing at the mountain top at Pisgah, seeing the city of palm trees, you may not

realize that the city is surrounded with fence, until you get very close. You might pursue a good dream, but keep in mind you will meet obstacles sometimes.

As we look at a Taste of Jericho, unlike Samaria that the people of God were actually living in, until things went bad. Jericho at this point represents where you are going to; it represents your dreams and aspirations. Jericho represents what you will like to see change. You have a glimpse of it, but not fully realized, because of a barrier, which we are going to look into. While Samaria may be your present situation, Jericho is the Future.

Joshua 2:1-10
Then Joshua the son of Nun sent two men as spies secretly from Shittim, saying, "Go, view the land, especially Jericho." So they went and came into the house of a harlot whose name was Rahab, and lodged there. It was told the king of Jericho, saying, "Behold, men from the sons of Israel have come here tonight to search out the land. And the king of Jericho sent word to Rahab, saying, "Bring out the men who have come to you, who have entered your house, for they have come to search out all the land. But the woman had taken the two men and hidden them, and she said, "Yes, the men came to me, but I did not know where they were from. It came about when it was time to shut the gate at dark, that the men went out; I do not know where the men went. Pursue them quickly, for you will overtake them." But she had brought them up to the roof and hidden them in the stalks of flax which she had laid in order on the roof. So the men pursued them on the road to the Jordan to the fords; and as soon as those who were pursuing them had gone out, they shut the gate. Now before they lay down, she came up to them on the roof, and said to the men,

I know that the LORD has given you the land, and that the terror of you has fallen on us, and that all the inhabitants of the land have melted away before you. For we have heard how the LORD dried up the water of the Red Sea before you when you came out of Egypt, and what you did to the two kings of the Amorites who were beyond the Jordan, to Sihon and Og, whom you utterly destroyed.

Jericho was very important to Joshua. There may be one thing you just need to get for your joy to be full; it is located in Jericho. There is no need to be afraid to take a step further. Do you know what the enemy has heard concerning you? Do you know what the enemy has heard concerning who you serve? It is possible that you are afraid to go to the city of palm trees, because you are afraid of the current inhabitants, yet the inhabitants of the city are even more afraid of you. You will never know, unless you dare to make a move.

Jericho is full of potentials. The fragrance was getting to them as they approached Jericho from Pisgah. It was the fragrance of opportunity; the fragrance of clean bill of health; the fragrance of children running and playing along the landscapes that they saw from Pisgah. The fragrance motivated the people to go. That same fragrance is restricting some people to go, because they cannot understand how it is possible to be so blessed, and so they are still standing at Pisgah saying, "this cannot be possible". We are standing at Pisgah, afraid to embrace greatness, afraid to receive the unrestricted access, not sure if we can handle success; they knew God is with them, they saw the greatness of God, but something else was missing.

(Joshua 5:1-15)

Joshua 6:1-5
Now Jericho was tightly shut because of the sons of Israel; no one went out and no one came in. The LORD said to Joshua, "See, I have given Jericho into your hand, with its king and the valiant warriors. You shall march around the city, all the men of war circling the city once. You shall do so for six days. Also seven priests shall carry seven trumpets of rams' horns before the ark; then on the seventh day you shall march around the city seven times, and the priests shall blow the trumpets. It shall be that when they make a long blast with the ram's horn, and when you hear the sound of the trumpet, all the people shall shout with a great shout; and the wall of the city will fall down flat, and the people will go up every man straight ahead.

What was missing? The gates of opportunity were shut; the gates of promotion were shut. The gates of safe environment for the children were shut. However, while the gates have been shut, we must see beyond those gates. God told him, don't worry about the physical gates that has been shut, I have delivered Jericho to you. I have given you unrestricted access to Joy, peace, promotion, breakthrough, but you must see beyond those gates to receive them.

There's a king in charge of your Jericho; there are fighting men in charge of your Jericho. It is time to take Jericho. It is time to make that move, but our hearts must be circumcised first, then we can have the unrestricted access to the city of palm tress.

Chapter Five

The Power of Imagination

"Imagination is everything. It is the preview of life's coming attractions" -Albert Einstein

Abraham was very old, and so was his wife, Sarah, when their son, Isaac was born, and the boy came as a promise to him. They had long since given up the dream of having a child. They had tried for several years, and had finally made their peace with it, until one beautiful quiet evening, his friend, the Almighty One showed up at his door and took him on a stroll to have a heart to heart conversation.
"What can you do for me now, am old, and so is my wife? I do not have children of my own, so a servant in my household will be my heir", Abraham said.
"Not so, my friend, not so, a son who is your own flesh and blood will be your heir". He answered.
Abraham, totally confused, looked at Him, but the Almighty One directed his eyes to the sky instead, and asked him to count the stars up there; as if he could really count that many stars. Then the Almighty One made him understand that as far as his heart can comprehend the stars above, so would his children be. At that point

Abraham began to see the images of millions of children; he began to image-a-nation of God's people, beginning with his own son, Isaac...

It is true that thoughts are based on logic and have limitations and rules; but imaginations are based on creativity, and have no limitations or rules. Your imaginations can save you, and it can also destroy you, if not properly managed.

Imagination is defined as the act or power of forming mental images of what is not actually present, or of what has never been actually experienced. Imaginations live off of faith in some aspects; but it is also possible for you to imagine without faith, or without believing. It is the powerful attributes of imaginations that makes it scary, if we don't really guide what we imagine.

"You can't depend on your eyes when your imagination is out of focus." — Mark Twain,

It is possible for two people to see exactly the same thing and have different reactions: it's all about how each one imagines that same thing.

How often do we work on our imaginations? *(Please understand that imagination is not daydreaming)*. How often do we spend some time to imagine what we have prayed for?

Ephesians 1:17-18 (CEB)
I pray that the God of our Lord Jesus Christ, the Father of glory, will give you a spirit of wisdom and revelation that

makes God known to you. I pray that the eyes of your heart will have enough light to see what is the hope of God's call, what is the richness of God's glorious inheritance among believers

It is possible for us to have a heart that desires, but have you been making use of the eyes that is located on the heart, and not on your face? Do you have enough light to see the hope of God's call? Have you harnessed enough of the power of imaginations? You can be operating on a shallow level, but to go deeper, you need enough light on the eyes of your heart.

Genesis 15:1-6
After this, the word of the Lord came to Abram in a vision: Do not be afraid, Abram. I am your shield, your very great reward. But Abram said, Sovereign Lord, what can you give me since I remain childless and the one who will inherit my estate is Eliezer of Damascus? And Abram said, You have given me no children; so a servant in my household will be my heir.
Then the word of the Lord came to him: This man will not be your heir, but a son who is your own flesh and blood will be your heir. He took him outside and said, Look up at the sky and count the stars, if indeed you can count them. Then he said to him, So shall your offspring be. Abram believed the Lord, and he credited it to him as righteousness.

God reminded Abraham that He is his shield, which means God is the one that is protecting him from attacks, and while He is doing that, He is also rewarding him greatly.

Abraham responded saying, "What good is this reward if I don't have anyone to pass the inheritance to? The only person to help me out is Eliezer of Damascus".

Abraham was using his physical eyes to see who will help him out. Eliezer of Damascus had been with Abraham, fought wars for him, gone on errands, check the cattle, etc., and so Abraham started building confidence in Eliezer of Damascus.

However, what we may or may not know is that Eliezer of Damascus is actually looking up to God for help. The name 'Eliezer' is a compound of two elements. The first part is the 'word', the common abbreviation of Elohim, meaning God. The second part comes from the verb 'azar', meaning help or support. So Eliezer actually means 'GOD IS MY HELP'. It is obvious that the eyes of Abraham's heart did not have enough light to see the hope of God's call and the richness of God's glorious inheritance.

God activated the power of imagination by asking Abraham to look up the sky and count the stars.

The first thing that came to Abram was the Word. The Word was necessary to jump start Abraham's inheritance. Thus, the Word is necessary to jump-start what you believe God for. For some people, the Word is enough, but for some other people, like Abraham and some of us, we need to go beyond just hearing the Word. The Word was specific and personal: *"A son who is your own Flesh and Blood"*. Abraham could not understand why God will say 'your own flesh and blood', when he was so old, and his wife was past the age of childbearing.

Verse 5: *"He took him outside and said, look up at the sky and count the stars, if indeed you can count them. Then he said to him, so shall your offspring be."*

God had to bring in the power of imagination. He took him outside beyond the boundaries of the physical eyes. God activated the power of imagination by asking Abraham to look up the sky and count the stars. So as Abraham looked up, there was enough light to enlighten the eyes of his heart, then he saw Isaac, and started counting from Isaac, to his grandchildren, to great grand children, until he simply lost count.

It was the Power of imagination that gave Abraham the audacity to take his only child for sacrifice; he had already seen something that goes beyond Isaac, and that made him confident.

****

Casting Down Imaginations

"Our weapons must be mighty through God and nothing else".

2 Corinthians 10:4-5
For the weapons of our warfare are not carnal, but mighty through God to the pulling down of strong holds: Casting down imaginations, and every high thing that exalteth itself against the knowledge of God, and bringing into captivity every thought to the obedience of Christ.

The above scripture was written partly because Paul was trying to defend his ministry. Let us examine why

Paul was trying to defend his ministry.

2Corinthians 10:1-18 (Read)

If you cannot define what you stand for, people will define it for you. Paul was a peculiar kind of person. He was a very shy person and most times, his writings have more weight than when you see him in person; he was a typical case of the pen mightier than the sword, so people began to judge him, trying to give him a standard, or expecting certain standards from him, which he needed to address, and that was the origin of the scripture above.

Probably the local Jewish newspaper, started to paint a picture of Paul, as people have started to paint a picture of you. They tweeted about the decisions you made, or you are about to make, but that does not define you as a person, or categorize you into something you are not. Thus, Paul was trying to tell the believers, we are not all the same. Paul was not a charismatic preacher that will keep you awake. As a matter of fact, one day, when he was preaching, he actually bored somebody to death; the guy fell off the window, but was resurrected again anyway.

However, he used this avenue to address certain things about what we go through and how we see things with our minds, and what must be done to address those issues.

2Corinthians 10:3
For though we walk in the flesh, we do not war according to

the flesh.

We don't have the same standard as the world does. The world uses physical weapons to fight; the world addresses some things from certain views, or certain angles, but I want us to know that our weapon is not a one-size fit all. Jesus healed three blind people differently. Some of our problems can be resolved with simple obedience; some might be resolved with a simple call to service; yet, some can be resolved by simple commitment.

2Corinthians 10:5
We are destroying speculations and every lofty thing raised up against the knowledge of God, and we are taking every thought captive to the obedience of Christ

Apostle Paul was talking about spiritual warfare. King James talks about the 'weapons are not carnal'; which means they are not physical, but mighty through God. So you can have a weapon that may be ordinary, and you can have a weapon that is mighty. You can also have a weapon that is mighty through knowledge, mighty through philosophy, mighty through science. One weapon that has been tested by Paul, used by believers, is the weapon that is mighty through only one means 'God'. Our weapon must be mighty through God; we cannot sidetrack God or push God aside when fighting a battle.

There are so many things embedded in this particular type of imagination that we must cast down: arguments, speculations, reasoning, intellectual arrogance, etc.

What does it mean to cast down? It means to destroy, to pull down, to discourage, or to reject. Whether you are a Christian or not, there are imaginations that will slow you down, if you don't destroy them.

Proverbs 4:20-23
My son, pay attention to what I say; turn your ear to my words. Do not let them out of your sight, keep them within your heart for they are life to those who find them and health to one's whole body. Above all else, guard your heart, for everything you do flows from it.

Proverb 4:23
Keep thy heart with all diligence for out of it are the issues of life.

It is what you pay attention to that will ultimately enter your heart, and will ultimately be processed. You become connected to what you pay attention to. Turn your ears to God's word. There are words flying around everywhere, your senses are picking up words, your eyes are picking up pictures, but we must make conscious effort to turn our ears to His words. It's the reason why the bible says, 'do not forsake the assembly of brethren', because the Word of God flows.

These days, many are turning their ears to something else; we turn our ears to the media, to fear. We are beginning to source for other things. Don't let His Word go out of your sight; don't let satan fulfil his ministry of stealing the Word of God from you. The bible says when you get the Word, keep them within your heart; because anything that is kept in your heart, whether hatred, malice, suicidal thoughts, killings, as well as making your self a better person, living in good health, promotion, success in every area, will eventually build up substance within the heart, which will eventually affect your imaginations enough to increase your faith or destroy your faith. This is why we must cast down imaginations that are based on the wrong foundation.

Some problems begin to magnify themselves above the knowledge of God. What are those thoughts that scare you? What are those thoughts that keep you awake at night? Some of these thoughts have reoccurred a thousand times over that you are now believing them; it is time to bring those thoughts and imaginations into captivity to the obedience of Christ.

Chapter Six

The Race Factor

"The truth must be sought after, looked for, identified, and verified before it can be activated"

Cameron always believed he is different from other people; most people love to drive cars, but he longs to race them. He learns about racing and the world around him by watching TV as a little boy, and then listening to the words of his best friend, Denny, an up and coming race car driver. Soon enough Cameron discovers that the Christian life is just like being on the race track; it is not simply about going fast. So, applying the rules of racing to his world, ensuring he was on the right track and that he was properly serviced and fuelled, Cameron takes on life's challenges, holding in his heart the dream that he will go on to be a champion in this race, and celebrate with the cloud of witnesses, the triumph of the human spirit when driven by God's Spirit.

Race is defined as competition between runners, horses, vehicles, boats, etc., to see which is the fastest in covering a set course. The key word in a race is a 'set course'. A set course is a predetermined route that has been spe-

cifically chosen by the organizers of the race to cover. So, for the purpose of this topic, our organizer, God, has chosen a set course.
Here, factor means circumstance, fact, or influence that contributes to a result, or outcome. Three significant factors here are: Circumstance, Fact, and Influence.

The race factor cannot be overlooked. Paul had this to say about it.
Galatians 2:2
I went in response to a revelation and, meeting privately with those esteemed as leaders, I presented to them the gospel that I preach among the Gentiles. I wanted to be sure I was not running and had not been running my race in vain.

After 14 years of preaching the Gospel, Paul did not look at how much his writings had transformed the Churches or the gentiles. After 14 years of divine guidance of the Holy Spirit, Paul did not want to neglect the race factor. Paul recognized that it is possible to overlook, or even neglect the race factor; he went in response to a revelation. The race factor was so important that God had to reveal to Paul, to go and meet with the leaders, to ensure he was on the right path, and was not running his race in vain.

Some of the things that will show up when considering the race factor like Paul said is: Humility, Tears, and Testing, which may be sometimes severe, and sometimes not so severe. These are the things that put us in check, reminding us why we are still in the race. For us not to forget the race factor, we must be on our guard.

The Factors

Earlier on I mentioned these three factors: circumstances, fact and influence. Taking a deeper look at these factors, I discovered that if you don't properly handle these three in a race, you would most likely lose the race.

1. **Circumstance:** Literally means that which stands around (something). You are better off standing above the circumstance than under the circumstance. If you allow your circumstance get into you, you will drown; if you shut your circumstance out, you will stay above.

2. **Facts:** *"There is nothing more deceptive than an obvious fact."* — Arthur Conan Doyle.
Most times we stop on the facts; we don't want to go the extra mile to where the truth that will set free is located. The truth is always behind the fact; and must be sought after, identified and verified before it can be activated. Don't live on the facts, search out the truth, and follow the truth, no matter what the facts are saying. Facts are temporal, truth is eternal, and so truth would keep you winning in the race.

3. **Influence:** A power affecting a person, thing, or course of events, especially one that operates without any direct or apparent effort. Is your past relationship affecting your marriage? Are your peers influencing you? The very thing that influences you owns you, and decides how far you go in this race of life.

****

Is there not a cause?

"Your circumstance has to do with a lot of what you tolerate"

1Samuel 17:26-29
Then David spoke to the men who were standing by him, saying, "What will be done for the man who kills this Philistine and takes away the reproach from Israel? For who is this uncircumcised Philistine, that he should taunt the armies of the living God? The people answered him in accord with this word, saying, "Thus it will be done for the man who kills him. Now Eliab his oldest brother heard when he spoke to the men; and Eliab's anger burned against David and he said, "Why have you come down? And with whom have you left those few sheep in the wilderness? I know your insolence and the wickedness of your heart; for you have come down in order to see the battle. But David said, "What have I done now? Was it not just a question?

David could not tolerate Mr. Goliath. He then looked for a reason for him to do what he had to do. He looked for a motivator to fight the enemy. You tend to stay longer in that situation if you cannot find a reason to get out. However, I want you to know that not all reasons are reasonable.

Reasons that will eventually destroy your trust in God are unreasonable. There was a group of people in the bible called the Galatians. The Galatians got stuck in a situation; a situation that was leaning more to trust on their laws, rather than trust in God. They were going back and forth, and Paul noticed that they were looking for a reason, but more to trust their laws, than God.

(Galatians 3:1-29)

We may look for reasons or a cause, but we must make sure it is reasonable, so that we don't be like the foolish Galatians. David did not abandon his job, but rather looked for an opportunity to either increase it, or better his life. If you don't get tired of where you are, you will not look for better opportunities.

1Corinthians 10:13
There hath no temptation taken you but such as is common to man: but God is faithful, who will not suffer you to be tempted above that ye are able; but will with the temptation also make a way to escape, that ye may be able to bear it.

Tasks that confront us, have limitations, it has what programmers call a back door. If we are stuck with a problem or task for a long time, then it probably means that we don't know how to look for a way of escape, or a back door to a problem. A way of escape is not a one-size fit all. A way of escape can come in the form of prophetic prayers and declaration. It can also come in the form of your service to God.

You have enough motive, enough reason to step up. There is always a way of escape

A way of escape can also be a combination of several things, like what David did. David, like every one of us, saw himself as a leader. He understood that leaders solve problems. One of the first tests to test if you will be a successful leader is the ability to solve problems. The more problems you solve, the more effective a leader you will become.

"Problems are only opportunities in work clothes"
—Henri Kaiser

'Is there not a cause?' is simply saying, you have enough motive, enough reason to step up. Remember, there is always a way of escape. ASK GOD.

****

The Value of Time and Chance

Ecclesiastes 9:11
I have seen something else under the sun: The race is not to the swift or the battle to the strong, nor does food come to the wise or wealth to the brilliant or favor to the learned; but time and chance happen to them all.

While Solomon was analyzing things, he saw something quite profound. When we take time to think and analyze, things will be revealed to us. "I have seen something else under the sun" means I have discovered something that is important. It means something has been revealed.

Solomon used the term, 'something else'; chances are this 'something' was probably there all along, but Solomon just discovered it, as he analyzed the circumstances. There is a possibility that there is something else attached to what you are looking at, you only need to search deeper. Solomon suddenly knew the truth, as he searched deeper.

Let us take a closer look at Jacob's dream at Bethel. **Gen 28:10-22** (Read)

Jacob had an experience on the ladder, with angels ascending and descending; then he saw something else, he discovered something else, he realized something else: "The Lord is in this place, and I knew it not". He looked beyond the fact to realize the truth, even though it didn't look too good. Brethren, it is possible that the Lord is in that problem with you, and you are just not realizing it.

Race, battle, food, and brilliance; these four things center around what we do, and what we want to achieve.

I'm very certain that was where Jacob got strength for the journey he was about to embark on, but he didn't stop there, he made a vow to God. What vows have you made to God that if He delivered you from your problem, you will do unto Him? When you make a vow to God, He expects you to perform your vow to Him.

Race, battle, food, and brilliance; these four things center around what we do, and what we want to achieve. We are in a race to achieve something; we want to be swift or quick at doing that. When we find ourselves fighting unseen forces, we want to be strong so that we can prevail. For us to enjoy the good things of life, we want to acquire wealth. What about knowing mysteries, having knowledge, gaining understanding, and being wise?

Time and chance was what took place in the episode of the Hunter and the tent man: this is referring to Esau and Jacob. We see Esau the skillful hunter, who knows how to run and pursue animals with so much strength; and then we see Jacob who was very calculative, waiting for the chance to get the birthright, but prepared ahead of time to rear the animals, instead of hunting every time he needed food.

The double portion of anointing Elisha received from Elijah (2kings2: 9-15), was based on time and chance.

Chapter Seven

The Conversation

"Before something happens to a nation, a conversation has taken place"

"Father, where are you taking me?"
The old man turned shakily upon his cane, paused at the top step and looked toward his daughter, while still panting to catch his breath. Despite the wrinkles that had lately etched their way across his face, she could still understand the sly smile that always signaled he's teasing her.
"Why, Esther, this is the place the Book of life is kept. You've been here a dozen times, and you still don't understand."
"Of course, Father, I know that"
As if to punctuate her statement, she glanced about the monument. Her gaze rose into the blue Judean sky, where the Sanctuary's celebrated dome thrust its odd, white swirl. She noted again its fluid shape; then suddenly, after all these years, understanding came to her that it was meant to evoke the ancient jar lids that once sealed the beloved Scrolls of the Word of God, now housed inside.

"How did I not understand this all along?' Esther wondered.

The same way we have physical conversations, we also have silent spiritual conversations daily that we may or may not be aware of, or even understand, though we hear it everyday. Some of these conversations we could hear in our spirit mind by way of intuition, or a nudging through the Holy Spirit.

Before something happens to a nation or a person, a conversation has taken place. Before something happens to a family, a conversation has taken place. A discussion must have taken place on your behalf concerning what you are petitioning God for, whether or not you know it.

Psalm 110:1-7
The LORD said unto my Lord, Sit thou at my right hand, until I make thine enemies thy footstool. The LORD shall send the rod of thy strength out of Zion: rule thou in the midst of thine enemies. Thy people shall be willing in the day of thy power, in the beauties of holiness from the womb of the morning: thou hast the dew of thy youth. The LORD hath sworn, and will not repent, Thou art a priest for ever after the order of Melchizedek. The Lord at thy right hand shall strike through kings in the day of his wrath. He shall judge among the heathen, he shall fill the places with the dead bodies; he shall wound the heads over many countries. He shall drink of the brook in the way: therefore shall he lift up the head.

The question is, do we always have knowledge of this conversation, and even if we have knowledge of it, do we understand the meaning of the conversation? Some conversations can be coded, while some are just plain. How do we decipher a coded conversation, if we have an opportunity to even hear it?

A Coded conversation took place in **Daniel 5:5-8**
Suddenly the fingers of a human hand appeared and wrote on the plaster of the wall, near the lampstand in the royal palace. The king watched the hand as it wrote. His face turned pale and he was so frightened that his legs became weak and his knees were knocking. The king summoned the enchanters, astrologers and diviners. Then he said to these wise men of Babylon, Whoever reads this writing and tells me what it means will be clothed in purple and have a gold chain placed around his neck, and he will be made the third highest ruler in the kingdom. Then all the king's wise men came in, but they could not read the writing or tell the king what it meant.

The output of this conversation came in form of the fingers of a human hand writing on the wall, which the king saw, as it was being written, but the king could not understand, neither did his magicians understand what it meant, because it was coded.

The first conversation that took place in the world was in **Genesis 1:26**.
Then God said, "Let us make mankind in our image, in our likeness, so that they may rule over the fish in the sea and the birds in the sky, over the livestock and all the wild animals, and over all the creatures that move along the ground.

The conversation in Psalm 110:1-7 can be understood and achieved, if we have a divine understanding of the conversation in Genesis. Psalm 110 is based on and dependent on the Genesis conversation. You will notice a trend in the beginning of Genesis that when God was creating the world, there was no mention of 'let us'. He just went ahead and did whatever He wanted. God did not have a conversation with anyone when He saw darkness. He did not have a conversation with anyone when He saw that the earth was without form. He did not have a conversation with anyone to separate the waters from the land; God did not have a conversation until in Verse 26, and that's when God said, *"let us make man in our own image in our own likeness"*.

> **The power to dominate is located in the likeness of God.**

Image is physical: what you see, and likeness is inward: what you don't see. Much of the power that God expects us to have is attached to His likeness; but most times we simply operate as an image, put up a front, just fine being physical, but we leave out the important part, which is the likeness. The power to dominate is located in the likeness of God. Please note that God requires our image to be decent, not haggard, not sorry looking; you can agree or disagree with me on this, but that is just my personal opinion. At times we see people who really want to be in His likeness, but they forget about His image part. We must represent both His image and His likeness to strike a balance in life, because we were created and designed to function both ways. The conversations about you and to you

> **We must represent both His image and His likeness to strike a balance in life, because we were created and designed to function both ways.**

become easier for you to understand when you operate in His image and in His likeness.

****

As the Lord Liveth

"Don't allow convenience to distract you".

Psalm 18:46-50
The LORD lives, and blessed be my rock; And exalted be the God of my salvation, The God who executes vengeance for me, And subdues peoples under me. He delivers me from my enemies; Surely You lift me above those who rise up against me; You rescue me from the violent man. Therefore I will give thanks to You among the nations, O LORD, And I will sing praises to Your name. He gives great deliverance to His king, And shows loving kindness to His anointed, To David and his descendants forever.

The beginning of Psalm 18 talks about the attributes of God and what God did in the life of David. David was trying to establish the Almighty nature of God. He wanted to establish a fact, and the attributes of God that will strengthen him and make him rely more on God. There is a need to bring yourself to acknowledge these attributes that made David to say "The Lord lives". Verse 46 declared that the Lord lives? Why do we need to know that the Lord lives?

An understanding of the Lord liveth will help you triumph over your enemies; it gives you a peace that passes all understanding, even when you are riding in the storm. After the establishments of these truths about God that He Lives, you will see the children of God in the bible, using this established truth about the nature of God to get their deliverance, or receive their petitions.

Several people, and the prophets in the bible had this understanding, and you begin to hear them say "As the Lord liveth.... " This statement, as simple as it may sound, is very powerful. It creates an atmosphere of miracle. As the Lord liveth activates the presence of God in any situation, no matter how hard the situation may be. As the Lord liveth is also used as an oath; if people want to validate whatever they stand for, they declare as the Lord liveth; therefore, it is like a seal that has been placed on something to authenticate it. As the Lord Liveth is used to acquire boldness and make pronouncements that you ordinarily cannot make, because you have activated the power of God before the declaration.

1Kings 17:1-9
Now Elijah the Tishbite, who was of the settlers of Gilead, said to Ahab, As the LORD, the God of Israel lives, before whom I stand, surely there shall be neither dew nor rain these years, except by my word. The word of the LORD came to him, saying, Go away from here and turn eastward, and hide yourself by the brook Cherith, which is east of the Jordan. It shall be that you will drink of the brook, and I have commanded the ravens to provide for you there. So he went and did according to the word of the LORD, for he went and lived by the brook Cherith, which is east of the Jordan. The ravens brought him bread and meat in the morning and bread and meat in the evening, and he would drink from the brook. It happened after a while that the brook dried up, because there

was no rain in the land. Then the word of the LORD came to him, saying, Arise, go to Zarephath, which belongs to Sidon, and stay there; behold, I have commanded a widow there to provide for you.

Sometimes in life we may have to make some declarations against the run of play. Some things may have developed into a pattern that we must break, like Elijah declared that which is undeniable - "the Lord liveth." This is a truth that is unquestionable; since God cannot die, then the problem has to die. As The Lord liveth is a statement that God cannot easily ignore.

2 kings 2:2
Elijah said to Elisha, "Stay here; the LORD has sent me to Bethel. But Elisha said, As surely as the LORD lives and as you live, I will not leave you. So they went down to Bethel.

Elijah was testing the authenticity of Elisha in terms of his calling; he wanted to know if Elisha was really chosen by God. Elijah caused a virtual distraction, but Elisha, through the acknowledgment that the Lord lives, said he couldn't be distracted. Don't allow convenience to distract you. Elisha was given a convenient way out, the harmless way out, to distract him, but he was too focused to be distracted, knowing that the Lord lives, so he cannot fail.

****

The Next Chapter
"The desire to move to the next chapter depends on you".
Ecclesiastes 3:1-8

There is a time for everything, and a season for every activity under the heavens: a time to be born and a time to die, a time to plant and a time to uproot, a time to kill and a time to heal, a time to tear down and a time to build, a time to weep and a time to laugh, a time to mourn and a time to dance, a time to scatter stones and a time to gather them, a time to embrace and a time to refrain from embracing, a time to search and a time to give up, a time to keep and a time to throw away, a time to tear and a time to mend, a time to be silent and a time to speak, a time to love and a time to hate, a time for war and a time for peace.

'God is Omniscient'. This term refers to the all-knowing nature of God. Webster dictionary defines it as, "the quality of knowing all things at once; universal knowledge; knowledge unbounded or infinite." God knows our very thoughts, our feelings, our desires, and our needs.

God has a book for everyone, and the book is made up of chapters.

Psalm 139: 16
Your eyes saw my unformed body; all the days ordained for me were written in your book before one of them came to be.

God has a book for everyone, and the book is made up of chapters. You have the ability to move to the next chapter and even change the outcome of the next chapter. Each activity located in Ecclesiastes 3 can be found in chapters, or sub chapters, and if you don't like the chapter you are in right now, you can correct it at the next chapter. We don't have control of verse 2: A time to be born and a time to die. However, I discovered that every one of us can be located in verse 2b to verse 8. Only you can determine how long you stay in a particular time and season. If the time and season that you are in right now is not favorable, and you want to leave that time and season, you are moving to the next chapter of your life.

If the time and season is good for you right now, God is saying the next chapter can be better than this present chapter. If you find yourself in a time and season of love, of course, you don't want to go to the chapter of hatred, but improve on the chapter of love. Remain in the time and season of love, because God is love, so you cannot go to the chapter of hatred.

A time to plant and a time to uproot: you may have been in the chapter of planting all these years; the next chapter is to harvest what you have planted.

A time to kill and a time to heal: you may be in the chapter of sickness, but the next chapter is healing.

A time to tear down and a time to build: things may have been bad, broken down in the chapter that you are in right now, the next chapter is to build up. What steps do you want to take to build up? What tools must you possess to help you build up? God is saying it's time to build up what has been torn down.

A time to weep and a time to laugh: have you been in the chapter of weeping where you have been crying every night to sleep? Well, I have good news for you; it's time for you to move to the next chapter of laughter.

A time to mourn and a time to dance: have you been

mourning over something you have lost in this chapter of your life, the next chapter is dancing.

A time to scatter stones and a time to gather them: does it look like you have been scattering stones, throwing away money? The next chapter is for gathering those things you have scattered.

A time to embrace and a time to refrain from embracing: what negative things have you been embracing? What have you attached yourself to that God does not want? Today is a good day of making that decision to move to the next chapter.

A time to search and a time to give up: have you been in the chapter of searching for the wrong things, move to the next chapter, and give up searching for the wrong things.

A time to keep and a time to throw away: what idols have you been keeping that prevents you from serving God? It's time to throw them away.

A time to tear and a time to mend: what are the things that have been torn in the chapter that you are in right now? It's time to mend them.

A time to be silent and a time to speak: have you been silent for too long in the chapter you are in right now? It's time to speak life, to speak progress, to speak freedom from captivity, etc.

A time for war and a time for peace: has it been a chapter of war, its time to say peace, be still.

A lot of where we are right now that does not look good can be changed, if we know what the next chapter is, and a lot depends on the decisions or choices we will make today. The analogy of the next chapter was seen in the lives of the Israelite when God spoke to them to go to the next chapter.

Deuteronomy 30:11-20
Now what I am commanding you today is not too difficult for you or beyond your reach. It is not up in heaven, so that you have to ask, "Who will ascend into heaven to get it and proclaim it to us so we may obey it?" Nor is it beyond the sea, so that you have to ask, "Who will cross the sea to get it and proclaim it to us so we may obey it?" No, the word is very near you; it is in your mouth and in your heart so you may obey it. See, I set before you today life and prosperity, death and destruction. For I command you today to love the LORD your God, to walk in obedience to him, and to keep his commands, decrees and laws; then you will live and increase, and the LORD your God will bless you in the land you are entering to possess. But if your heart turns away and you are not obedient, and if you are drawn away to bow down to other gods and worship them, I declare to you this day that you will certainly be destroyed. You will not live long in the land you are crossing the Jordan to enter and possess. This day I call the heavens and the earth as witnesses against you that I have set before you life and death, blessings and curses. Now choose life, so that you and your children may live and that you may love the LORD your God, listen to his voice, and hold fast to him. For the LORD is your life, and he will give you many years in the land he swore to give to your fathers, Abraham,

Isaac and Jacob.

God is simply saying take that bold step to the next chapter of your life. If you are in a chapter that is good, God is saying improve or expand on that chapter.

Chapter Eigth

The Path to Greatness: The Seed
"The path to greatness starts with a seed"

Matthew 13:1-9
That day Jesus went out of the house and was sitting by the sea. And large crowds gathered to Him, so He got into a boat and sat down, and the whole crowd was standing on the beach. And He spoke many things to them in parables, saying, Behold, the sower went out to sow; and as he sowed, some seeds fell beside the road, and the birds came and ate them up. Others fell on the rocky places, where they did not have much soil; and immediately they sprang up, because they had no depth of soil. But when the sun had risen, they were scorched; and because they had no root, they withered away. Others fell among the thorns, and the thorns came up and choked them out. And others fell on the good soil and yielded a crop, some a hundredfold, some sixty, and some thirty. He who has ears, let him hear.

A seed is a plant's unit of reproduction, capable of developing into another such plant.
Greatness is defined as the quality of being great, distinguished, or eminent.

Jesus went out of the house and sat down beside the lake, something serious was about to be done: a generation of people was about to be placed on the path to Greatness. It was from here that Jesus started talking about the Kingdom of God. He looked at the crowd and saw people that were given the same opportunities, but they utilized it differently.

A farmer went out to scatter seed; we know that any farmer has one intention, and that is to get a great harvest. Farmers do not go out to plant seed or scatter seed so that the seeds can be destroyed. Farmers that are looking for fruits know the value of sowing the seed. The seed was the message of the Kingdom; thus, it was very significant for Jesus to start with that parable about the message of the kingdom. The seed was scattered to everyone. here, the Word you hear is the seed, the message of the kingdom.

Jesus looked at the crowd and saw each of their status spiritually; Jesus saw that at one point in their lives, they have received seed that the farmer had gone out to scatter. He discovered that these seed that was scattered depends a whole lot on the status of the people spiritually. He wanted to place them on a journey to greatness, but discovered that the path to greatness starts with a seed, and how that seed is treated.

Four Places were identified where each of us could be standing spiritually:
1. **Beside the Road:** This side of the road referred to in this scripture talks about those of us who are what I call 'onlookers.' God did not create us to be onlookers in His

kingdom. Some of us do not want the responsibility of doing meaningful work for God. God is not interested in your work for Him, but He is interested in your meaningful work.

2. **Rocky ground:** These are the ones the bible says have no roots, and cannot really grow, because rocky grounds are often infertile. When trees have no deep roots, they get uprooted and die when there's a slight wind. So Jesus saw some of these people standing on the rocky ground. Some of us fall into this category. These people are excited about the seed, they want to hear what the seed has done for somebody; they will like to have an encounter, so that the seed can develop into fruits, but they don't want to get themselves dirty with the soil. They don't want to roll up their sleeves to do the work required. They fall every time there is trouble, because there is no deep root, and growth does not occur due to infertile ground.

3. **The Thorns:** The bible describes some as standing with thorns. Someone who hears the Word, but allows the worries of this life and the deceitfulness of wealth choke the word, making it unfruitful.

4. **The Good soil:** This is where we should be standing. The good soil makes the seed thrive, and develop into a great tree. Being on the good soil is the right path that leads to greatness; the soil is fertile, and so everything grows and thrives.

****

An Enemy Hath Done this
"There is a difference between an enemy and the enemy".

Matthew 13:9-29 (Read)

We see Jesus teaching the People the path to Greatness. Where you are standing determines what will happen to the seed. Some are standing by the way side; some are standing on the rocky grounds; some are in the midst of thorns; and some are on the good ground.

The good ground is where we can get a hundred fold. The good ground is when you have made up your mind to serve wholeheartedly. The good ground is where we are all encouraged to stand. Some of us know how to stand by the good ground; and some of us have been standing by the good ground for some time.

After talking about the other people on how to step into the path to greatness, Jesus then decided to talk to the 'Good ground' people, because there were some good ground people listening to him, while he spoke in parables. Jesus saw them and knew they are doing well, but He needed to let them know about somebody called 'An Enemy'.

The good ground people knew 'The Enemy', but they did not know 'An Enemy'.
There is a difference between An Enemy and The enemy. The Enemy is that which you know; An Enemy may not be known until they strike you. The Enemy has certain characteristics or features that you can use to iden-

tify them, but an enemy is usually disguised. The Enemy makes noise when he is coming, but An Enemy is silent. However, when The Enemy sees that he cannot get you, he changes to An Enemy.

An Enemy can be external or internal. Though the path to greatness starts with a seed, it can be aligned with An Enemy at different stages in life.

Mark 10:17-31
As He was setting out on a journey, a man ran up to Him and knelt before Him, and asked Him, "Good Teacher, what shall I do to inherit eternal life? And Jesus said to him, Why do you call Me good? No one is good except God alone. You know the commandments, 'DO NOT MURDER, DO NOT COMMIT ADULTERY, DO NOT STEAL, DO NOT BEAR FALSE WITNESS, Do not defraud, HONOR YOUR FATHER AND MOTHER. And he said to Him, "Teacher, I have kept all these things from my youth up. Looking at him, Jesus felt a love for him and said to him, "One thing you lack: go and sell all you possess and give to the poor, and you will have treasure in heaven; and come, follow Me. But at these words he was saddened, and he went away grieving, for he was one who owned much property. And Jesus, looking around, said to His disciples, How hard it will be for those who are wealthy to enter the kingdom of God! The disciples were amazed at His words. But Jesus answered again and said to them, "Children, how hard it is to enter the kingdom of God! It is easier for a camel to go through the eye of a needle than for a rich man to enter the kingdom of God. They were even more astonished and said to Him, "Then who can be saved? Looking at them, Jesus said, With people it is impossible, but not with God; for all things are possible with God.

Peter began to say to Him, "Behold, we have left everything and followed You. Jesus said, Truly I say to you, there is no one who has left house or brothers or sisters or mother or father or children or farms, for My sake and for the gospel's sake, but that he will receive a hundred times as much now in the present age, houses and brothers and sisters and mothers and children and farms, along with persecutions; and in the age to come, eternal life. But many who are first will be last, and the last, first.

This rich man could understand how to avoid The Enemy, but could not handle An Enemy. Lets compare this rich man with another rich man called Elisha:

1kings 19:19-21
So he departed from there and found Elisha the son of Shaphat, while he was plowing with twelve pairs of oxen before him, and he with the twelfth. And Elijah passed over to him and threw his mantle on him. He left the oxen and ran after Elijah and said, "Please let me kiss my father and my mother, then I will follow you. And he said to him, Go back again, for what have I done to you? So he returned from following him, and took the pair of oxen and sacrificed them and boiled their flesh with the implements of the oxen, and gave it to the people and they ate. Then he arose and followed Elijah and ministered to him.

Elisha knew that there was something greater than his riches. He knew how to confront An Enemy and The Enemy. He slaughtered his oxen, his wealth, roasted them with his equipment, and gave all to the people to eat, to ensure he does not even get tempted to return to his business; and he followed a greater calling. So we see two rich people, one could not confront An Enemy, and the other confronted An enemy.

****

The Field and the Fine Pearls
"Treasure is what you value".

Matthew 13:34-45
Then He left the crowds and went into the house. And His disciples came to Him and said, "Explain to us the parable of the tares of the field. And He said, "The one who sows the good seed is the Son of Man, and the field is the world; and as for the good seed, these are the sons of the kingdom; and the tares are the sons of the evil one; and the enemy who sowed them is the devil, and the harvest is the end of the age; and the reapers are angels. So just as the tares are gathered up and burned with fire, so shall it be at the end of the age. The Son of Man will send forth His angels, and they will gather out of His kingdom all stumbling blocks, and those who commit lawlessness, and will throw them into the furnace of fire; in that place there will be weeping and gnashing of teeth. Then THE RIGHTEOUS WILL SHINE FORTH AS THE SUN in the kingdom of their Father. He who has ears, let him hear. The kingdom of heaven is like a treasure hidden in the field, which a man found and hid again; and from joy over it he goes and sells all that he has and buys that field. The kingdom of heaven is like a treasure hidden in the field, which a man found and hid again; and from joy over it he goes and sells all that he has and buys that field.

Proverbs 2:1-5

My son, if you will receive my words. And treasure my commandments within you, Make your ear attentive to wisdom, Incline your heart to understanding; For if you cry for discernment, Lift your voice for understanding; If you seek her as silver, And search for her as for hidden treasures; Then you will discern the fear of the LORD, And discover the knowledge of God.

There will be times when we need to remember some things as we move along this path to greatness to enable us unlock a treasure, or to find something of value. My favorite book in the bible, Proverbs, says, *"If you accept my words and store up my commandments within you…"* There are several 'Ifs', which is a conditional statement. In computer programming, a conditional statement only holds true or false value. We must meet the conditions of all the 'Ifs' to get the positive value. The Message Bible Version says we should guard the counsels of the Lord with our life; tune our ears to the word of wisdom. This means that there are many stations out there available to people, free of charge. We have the power to listen to whatever station we want to listen to.

> **We must meet the conditions of all the 'Ifs' to get the positive value.**

Verse 4 is very critical, it says, "If you seek her as silver, and search for her as for hidden treasures," which means searching for it like a prospector panning for gold, like an adventurer on a treasure hunt.

Mathew 13:35 declare, *"I will utter things hidden since the creation of the world"*. As we walk in the path to greatness, we will come to a place called Treasure Island. Treasure Island is an Island where treasures have been hidden since the creation of the world. Treasure Island is a place of discovery, a place of confirmation. Treasure Island was designed not for you to stumble into it, but for you to purposely look for and discover it.

Isaiah 45:3 says,
And I will give thee the treasures of darkness, and hidden riches of secret places.

Why would there be treasures of darkness? Why would there be riches of secret places? Is it possible to say we are children of God and heirs to the throne without us discovering the treasures in secret places?

Treasure is not limited to jewelry, money, or riches alone. Treasure is what you value most. In other words, if your health is of value you will treasure it; if your job is of value, you will treasure it; if your business is of value you will treasure it; if your family is of value you will treasure them, etc. We have different things that is of value to us, and whether we like it or not, we treasure them. What you don't value, you will misuse or abuse.

Treasures of Darkness and hidden riches of secret places are not designed for us to easily see it. There's a reason why it's called 'riches in secret places'. Sometimes, the place you are looking at may have already been discovered, so it is no longer hidden, and that is why you are not progressing in that business or that idea. Look for other secret places. The secret places cannot be exhausted.

Mathew 13:44-46
The kingdom of heaven is like treasure hidden in a field. When a man found it, he hid it again, and then in his joy went and sold all he had and bought that field. Again, the kingdom of heaven is like a merchant looking for fine pearls. When he found one of great value, he went away and sold everything he had and bought it.

I want to focus for a minute on the field, which is defined as an area of open land, especially one planted with crops or pasture, typically bound by hedges or fences. This particular field was not elaborated on in the bible; but if a field is an open land, how then can you hide a treasure in this open land? These treasures can easily be hidden in an open field, if the treasure has been camouflaged like the field. So, if you are stuck in the process of just looking without searching, you may miss the treasure.

> **If you are stuck in the process of just looking without searching, you may miss the treasure.**

More so, if crops have been planted in the field, and they have grown, will it not be easy to hide a treasure in the bushes? My answer is yes. God is wiser than us, and He said my thoughts towards you are thoughts of peace and not of evil, to give you an expected end. So let's assume this field has all types of plants and animals roaming around everywhere, let's take a look at this scenario:

Firstly, don't forget that God created the field for a reason, to bless us and for us to be a blessing to others; and so this field becomes the field of God. This field has lots of fruit, which needs to be catered for. This field now has sheep and lambs that now become our responsibilities. As we put on our work clothes to work for God in this field of God, whether as choir, usher, or Sunday school teacher, we go through this field daily, we stay and make sure all is put in place, and that this work does not suffer. We are consistent with our giving to promote the work. We make a decision to stay on the path to greatness, we begin to move around the field, and then all of a sudden we discover health, utilize its fruit, and while we are still eating the fruit of health, still working in the field, we discover finance, deliverance, and breakthrough; our lights begin to shine, we begin to think of expanding this field, the more we expand the more treasures we discover.

All this simply means is that the more we work the more the Holy Spirit drops something in your heart that will cause you to excel. Joshua knew the value in the field (Joshua 24), and he declared to his people that as for him and his household, they would serve the Lord.

What about the fine pearls?
Verse 45-46 *Again, the kingdom of heaven is like a merchant looking for fine pearls. When he found one of great value, he went away and sold everything he had and bought it.*

It has been said over and over again that these fine Pearls is talking about Jesus; sell all you have and follow Jesus, but I don't agree with that. A merchant comes seeking pearls and finds one of great value. In order to obtain it, he must sell all that he has to buy it. This Merchant is Jesus and this pearl is you and I, the Church. Jesus was telling us two things at the same time in the parable and that's why it's a parable anyway. The merchant, Jesus comes looking for a pearl and when he finds one of great value, when he finds one doing His will, when He finds one that though they are passing through troubles, they are still saying the Lord is on the throne, when He finds one who is on the brink of loosing his entire savings or even lost his entire savings, and yet glorifies God.... Jesus gives everything He has to buy these ones.

Chapter Nine

Non-Disclosure Agreement

"A lot of us have been in trouble or still in trouble because of the spiritual Babylonians that we told our most vulnerable secrets"

When life is at its best, one wrong word to one wrong person can shatter everything. Abigail had no reason to feel anything, but joy on the very morning her life became a nightmare. The epitome of the successful Jewish woman, she is married to a well-known and respected Doctor, and is in the middle of planning her daughter, Maria's wedding. Maria wakes up that morning with the world in the palm of her hand. Having lived the charmed life of a much-loved child from a happy family, she is a smart, beautiful Harvard Law student, who has never really questioned the path she found herself on.
However, with a shocking suddenness, all that is smashed to pieces in ways none of them could never have dreamt; all of Maria's dream came crashing right before her, all for one little story her mother unassumingly shared with her best friend of many years.

Isaiah 39:1-8
At that time Merodach-baladan son of Baladan, king of Bab-

ylon, sent letters and a present to Hezekiah, for he heard that he had been sick and had recovered. Hezekiah was pleased, and showed them all his treasure house, the silver and the gold and the spices and the precious oil and his whole armory and all that was found in his treasuries. There was nothing in his house nor in all his dominion that Hezekiah did not show them. Then Isaiah the prophet came to King Hezekiah and said to him, "What did these men say, and from where have they come to you?" And Hezekiah said, "They have come to me from a far country, from Babylon. He said, "What have they seen in your house?" So Hezekiah answered, "They have seen all that is in my house; there is nothing among my treasuries that I have not shown them. Then Isaiah said to Hezekiah, "Hear the word of the LORD of hosts, Behold, the days are coming when all that is in your house and all that your fathers have laid up in store to this day will be carried to Babylon; nothing will be left,' says the LORD. And some of your sons who will issue from you, whom you will beget, will be taken away, and they will become officials in the palace of the king of Babylon. Then Hezekiah said to Isaiah, The word of the LORD which you have spoken is good. For he thought, For there will be peace and truth in my days.

There are things that the Lord will require a non-disclosure agreement to be signed between Him and us. The word non-disclosure comes at a time when something is about to happen. This word is tied partially to His promises concerning us. There are certain things God wants us to say or testify about, but there are also things that God does not want us to say, especially if the enemy can use it against us.

In the scripture we read, we see a king and a prophet

engaged in a dialogue that involved the visit from another king. It is important to note that this visit is not just from any king, but the king of Babylon at that time. Babylon represents the enemy, who will not want to see the progress of the children of God. Babylon represents the one that comes as a friend, but is really a wolf in sheep clothing. Babylon also represents the one that looks like he or she is close to you, but is actually targeting the things of value to you, asking you questions on things that you are not supposed to be telling them. A lot of us have been in trouble or still in trouble because of the spiritual Babylonians that we told our most vulnerable secrets.

> **If we want to protect what we have, we must be able to spot a Merodach Balladan.**

There is an unleashing of a king called, Merodach Baladan. God is telling us that we must come to a place where we can recognize Merodach Baladan. As long as there is Babylon, there will always be a Merodach Baladan. If we want to progress in life, we must be aware of Merodach Balladan; if we want to protect what we have, we must be able to spot a Merodach Balladan.

It was a crucial time for King Hezekiah, who became sick unto death, but God reversed the sickness, and gave him more years to live; thus, it was a time of celebrations and jubilation. Statistics reveal that we are most vulnerable when we are celebrating, or rejoicing; we tend to drop down our guards. We forget that there are some things we should not disclose, but because we are so happy, we tell our enemies our secret without even knowing it.

Proverbs 21:23
He who guards his mouth and his tongue keeps himself from troubles.

Before we continue I want to talk about this king of Babylon named Merodach–Baladan:
Merodach-Baladan means the son of death. Merodach was a Babylonian idol, the god of war. Merodach-Baladan became the king of Babylon, and we know that the Babylonians are constantly tormenting the children of God, especially at a time when the son of death was now in charge of Babylon.

What are the spiritual implications of Merodach-Baladan?
*We cannot ignore a possibility of Merodach–Baladan assigned to our breakthroughs. In other words, God wants us to be on our guard, because of the Merodach-Baladans of this world, if he is not already taking advantage of us, then he is approaching us to get some information.
*A Merodach-Baladan's aim is to determine the areas of our vulnerabilities. Where can he hit us to make the maximum impact?
*Merodach-Baladan has a way of reasoning; 'if I cannot stop the blessings, if I cannot delay the promises, then I can look for the areas that they are weak and try to attack and destroy from there.'

The bible says, **2Corinthians 2:11**
Lest Satan should get an advantage of us: for we are not ignorant of his devices.

Though Paul was talking about forgiveness in this scripture, we discover that the word 'devices', which means more than one, can and may be used against the people of God. Hence, disclosure is one of the devices of the enemy. Disclosure exposes us to the enemy, and becomes what the enemy can use to attract and eventually get us. What have you disclosed to someone innocently, but it has been used to attack you? What treasures have you disclosed to the enemy, like King Hezekiah did?

When we begin to speak without thinking, it becomes a problem.

Disclosure comes easily to those who talk too much; you freely disclose information that they asked you, the one they didn't ask you, and the one they will ask you. When we begin to speak without thinking, it becomes a problem. Not everyone is a Merodach, because you still have to speak to someone about issues you are facing, so that they can help you, but there is an in-built sensor in us that always trigger on when there is a Merodach in front of us, many times we ignore those sensors.

The visit from Merodach-Baladan looked like a sign of relief from the Assyrians. Hezekiah did not know that he was being visited by an idol that was looking for his treasures. Without consulting the Lord or the Prophet Isaiah, he showed them his vast treasures, his abundant supplies of food, and his military armaments. God had given Hezekiah great wealth, so the visitors were duly impressed (2 Chron. 32:27-29). Hezekiah thought he could get protection against the Assyrians from the Babylonian king, he didn't know that he had a better protection, without the Babylonian king. God is speaking to someone today; what you think you need help for is not an issue, don't expose yourself to trouble!

****

The Trojan Horse
"Friends by day, enemies by night."

The Trojan horse physically looks friendly, but has the enemy inside. Anyone who tends to be friendly towards you, but inside is plotting your downfall is known as the Trojan horse. As we step out in faith doing great things, God is telling us to beware of Trojan horses, beware of mixed multitude.

Exodus 12:37-38
Then the children of Israel journeyed from Rameses to Succoth, about six hundred thousand men on foot, besides children. A mixed multitude went up with them also.

Numbers 11:4
Now the mixed multitude who were among them yielded to intense craving; so the children of Israel also wept again and said: "Who will give us meat to eat?

The mixed multitude that followed them from Egypt yielded to intense craving. The mixed multitude has been with them for some time; they were the ones who yielded, but influenced the Israelites to do the complaining.

Nehemiah 13:1-9
On that day they read aloud from the book of Moses in the

hearing of the people; and there was found written in it that no Ammonite or Moabite should ever enter the assembly of God, because they did not meet the sons of Israel with bread and water, but hired Balaam against them to curse them. However, our God turned the curse into a blessing. So when they heard the law, they excluded all foreigners from Israel. Now prior to this, Eliashib the priest, who was appointed over the chambers of the house of our God, being related to Tobiah, had prepared a large room for him, where formerly they put the grain offerings, the frankincense, the utensils and the tithes of grain, wine and oil prescribed for the Levites, the singers and the gatekeepers, and the contributions for the priests. But during all this time I was not in Jerusalem, for in the thirty-second year of Artaxerxes king of Babylon I had gone to the king. After some time, however, I asked leave from the king, and I came to Jerusalem and learned about the evil that Eliashib had done for Tobiah, by preparing a room for him in the courts of the house of God. It was very displeasing to me, so I threw all of Tobiah's household goods out of the room. Then I gave an order and they cleansed the rooms; and I returned there the utensils of the house of God with the grain offerings and the frankincense.

What gates have we opened for the enemy to come in? What relationship have we started that has opened the gate for the Trojan horse to come in? Eliashib was closely related to Tobiah, and removed the things of God to situate him instead, thereby causing offence. Who are you closely related to that knows your weaknesses, and he is using it against you? Let's purge every Trojan Horses in our lives.

****

Understanding by the Books

"Some of us are struggling, because of what we didn't take care of in the first year."

Daniel 1:1-20

Verse 1-7: *Then the king ordered Ashpenaz, the chief of his officials, to bring in some of the sons of Israel, including some of the royal family and of the nobles, youths in whom was no defect, who were good-looking, showing intelligence in every branch of wisdom, endowed with understanding and discerning knowledge, and who had ability for serving in the king's court; and he ordered him to teach them the literature and language of the Chaldeans. The king appointed for them a daily ration from the king's choice food and from the wine which he drank, and appointed that they should be educated three years, at the end of which they were to enter the king's personal service. Now among them from the sons of Judah were Daniel, Hananiah, Mishael and Azariah. Then the commander of the officials assigned new names to them; and to Daniel he assigned the name Belteshazzar, to Hananiah Shadrach, to Mishael Meshach and to Azariah Abed-nego...,*

Verse 18-20: *Then at the end of the days which the king had specified for presenting them, the commander of the officials presented them before Nebuchadnezzar. The king talked with them, and out of them all not one was found like Daniel, Hananiah, Mishael and Azariah; so they entered the king's personal service. As for every matter of wisdom and understanding about which the king consulted them, he found them ten times better than all the magicians and conjurers who were in all his realm.*

An instruction was given to Ashpenaz, chief of the eunuchs to educate and train the finest of Israel's young men. When one is called a eunuch, it means they cannot reproduce. Eunuchs don't have purposes in life; so they do not have anything to live for, and nothing to lose.

The question is why would a eunuch be used to train the best young men in captivity? The king figured that the best way to destroy the seed of greatness of those in captivity is to make sure they don't make progress in life; what better way to do that than to use someone who has nothing to lose and nothing to live for, so he can unleash every form of evil to utterly break and destroy them, even when it means destroying himself in the process. So the king sends the eunuch Ashpenaz; thus Ashpenaz becomes what I call a 'monitoring spirit'; a poison coated candy. The main strategy of Ashpenaz is to change their identity. He gave them different names, new identities; this ensures they can never be found by anyone looking for them; they cannot be traced.

As a result of disclosure by King Hezekiah to Merodach-Baldan many years ago, Jerusalem was besieged, and these promising young men were captured. Here, we see a situation where the consequences of the actions of a king, so many years ago is now rearing its ugly head. This is a typical case of *'our fathers have eaten sour grapes and the teeth of the children are set on edge'* (Ezekiel 18:2b). A whole nation went into captivity, until one day, a young man called, Daniel began to make inquiries.

Dan 9:1-6
In the first year of Darius the son of Ahasuerus, of the seed of the Medes, which was made king over the realm of the Chaldeans; In the first year of his reign I Daniel understood by books the number of the years, whereof the word of the LORD came to Jeremiah the prophet, that he would accomplish seventy years in the desolations of Jerusalem. And I set my face unto the Lord God, to seek by prayer and supplications, with fasting, and sackcloth, and ashes: And I prayed unto the LORD my God, and made my confession, and said, O Lord, the great and dreadful God, keeping the covenant and mercy to them that love him, and to them that keep his commandments; We have sinned, and have committed iniquity, and have done wickedly, and have rebelled, even by departing from thy precepts and from thy judgments: Neither have we hearkened unto thy servants the prophets, which spake in thy name to our kings, our princes, and our fathers, and to all the people of the land.

All the time Daniel was in captivity, he did not sit easy lamenting, he was searching the books for an answer, a way out of this captivity, knowing they have become untraceable; and finally he found what he needed to break through. As soon as understanding came to him, Daniel believed and accepted that every problem has a shelf life. In other words, every problem has an expiration date, and it is time to be free. That first year was very significant, as Daniel turned to God to confess their sins,

> **Search the books and discover what it says about your situation; that problem has an expiry date...**

and remind God of His covenant and mercy to them that love Him.

Some of us are struggling, because of what we didn't take care of in the first year. It is time to discover and know the truth, for it is only the truth that you know that really makes you free from all the struggles of life, not the truth you do not know, or the truth you cannot bring yourself to believe. Search the books and discover what it says about your situation; that problem has an expiry date written on it; God has not given up on you, His covenant and mercy is still active.

Chapter Ten

When the Nations are Raging

"Why do the heathen rage and the people imagine a vain thing"
- Psalm 2:2

David slumped to the ground and cried out in anguish: 'why do the heathen rage?...' It is a question, but it is also much more than a question. David expresses his horror, his astonishment, his amazement. He says, "Why are things like this... so much trouble?" From the first days to the closing days of the battle, from the first penetration of the Israeli line to the Philistine last desperate charge in the battle, David fought in the thickest of the action, helping take over the enemy territories. Though David and his men survived the battle, they had the victory over yet another nation of enemies, David felt not like a conqueror or a victor, but an exhausted survivor, left with his life and overwhelmed with emotions; it's been one battle to the next; it seems endless, and trouble is constantly brewing around him. How much longer before the heart of another nation, or person would be stirred once more against him? Yet, in all of it, the Lord of hosts says, *"be strong and courageous. You are more than a conqueror. I have given you the victory."* And it was a promise that was always dramatically fulfilled in his life each time.

Acts 3:1-9
One day Peter and John were going up to the temple at the time of prayer—at three in the afternoon. Now a man who was lame from birth was being carried to the temple gate called Beautiful, where he was put every day to beg from those going into the temple courts. When he saw Peter and John about to enter, he asked them for money. Peter looked straight at him, as did John. Then Peter said, Look at us! So the man gave them his attention, expecting to get something from them. Then Peter said, Silver or gold I do not have, but what I do have I give you. In the name of Jesus Christ of Nazareth, walk. Taking him by the right hand, he helped him up, and instantly the man's feet and ankles became strong. He jumped to his feet and began to walk. Then he went with them into the temple courts, walking and jumping, and praising God. When all the people saw him walking and praising God, they recognized him as the same man who used to sit begging at the temple gate called Beautiful, and they were filled with wonder and amazement at what had happened to him.

Acts 4:23-31
On their release, Peter and John went back to their own people and reported all that the chief priests and the elders had said to them. When they heard this, they raised their voices together in prayer to God. "Sovereign Lord," they said, you made the heavens and the earth and the sea, and everything in them. You spoke by the Holy Spirit through the mouth of your servant, our father David: "Why do the nations rage and the peoples plot in vain?" The kings of the earth rise up and the rulers band together against the Lord and against his

anointed one. Indeed Herod and Pontius Pilate met together with the Gentiles and the people of Israel in this city to conspire against your holy servant Jesus, whom you anointed. They did what your power and will had decided beforehand should happen. Now, Lord, consider their threats and enable your servants to speak your word with great boldness. Stretch out your hand to heal and perform signs and wonders through the name of your holy servant Jesus. After they prayed, the place where they were meeting was shaken. And they were all filled with the Holy Spirit and spoke the word of God boldly.

Something happened in the life of a man in Acts 3 that made Peter and John to remember what David said in **Psalm 2:2**
Why do the heathen rage, and the people imagine a vain thing?

A question was asked; 'why do they rage, why do they imagine a vain thing?' David looked at his situation, and discovered a pattern going on with his life.

The nations rage, because your success, or growth enrages the devil; each time your seed grows, his ego is badly bruised...

He remembered the time Saul threw a Javelin at him, trying to kill him for no reason. He remembered when he had to go hide at Cave Adullam in the cold, with no food or water. David constantly saw himself in and out of trouble, and at every point, God delivered him. Sometimes he suffers defeat, sometimes he suffers pain, and sometimes he does not know his left from his right. The nations were constantly tormenting him; the system of government was harsh on him, and God still showed up for him each time. However, the question remains, why do the heathen rage and the people imagine a vain thing?

To Rage means violent, uncontrollable anger. Vain means having no real value, idle, worthless. So, why so much anger over nothing? When your healing comes, the nations will rage. When your deliverance comes the nations will rage; and when your breakthrough comes, the nations will rage. The nations rage, because your success, or growth enrages the devil; each time your seed grows, his ego is badly bruised, that is annoying for him.

What do you do when the nations are raging? How can you withstand the raging of the Nations? Acts 3 gives us an insight to what happened at a time when healing came to someone.

The spiritual implication of being lame is that you cannot go far in life; we may be walking around with our two feet, yet we are not going far in life. As long as we don't go far in life, the nations will be fine. As long as we are confined within a boundary, the nations will be fine. This man was lame, and was carried to a place called Beautiful Gate. He was a man who got caught up in a system where he just had enough to survive. Some of us understand what I am saying; today most people are caught up in a system whereby if you miss one Pay Check, you will be in trouble.

However, there was something significant that I discovered about this gate called Beautiful. The Greek adjective used to name the gate, *'hōraios'*, can be defined as 'happening or coming at the right time; and also seen as 'beautiful, fair, or lovely'. In other words, this gate called Beautiful actually means 'Happening'. It's a place where things happen, a ripe place, coming at the right time. So this man had been coming to a place that has already been identified as ripe, the right time, without him knowing it. Then one day, Peter and John were passing by, they stopped and told him look at us. That moment of engagement was the moment of activation. It is possible that we have been coming to a place where things happen, yet nothing significant is happening to us, because we are not paying attention.

"The moment one gives close attention to any thing, even a blade of grass, it becomes a mysterious, awesome, indescribably magnificent world in itself. - Henry Miller

An interesting thing happened in **Job 33:8-33**, but let us look at **Verse 32-33**
If you have anything to say, answer me; speak up, for I want to vindicate you. But if not, then listen to me; be silent, and I will teach you wisdom.

Isaiah 42:20
You have seen many things, but you pay no attention; your ears are open, but you do not listen.

God may have shown you many things in the past, He may have told you many things too, but today He is asking you to pay attention.

****

The Face of a Mirage

"The harvest is past, the summer has ended, and we are not saved."

Jeremiah 8:20-22
The harvest is past, the summer has ended, and we are not saved. Since my people are crushed, I am crushed; I mourn, and horror grips me. Is there no balm in Gilead? Is there no physician there? Why then is there no healing for the wound of my people?

A Mirage is an optical illusion caused by atmospheric conditions. An optical illusion is characterized by visually perceived images that are deceptive or misleading.

Jeremiah had a reputation like Elijah. He had a purpose to reveal the sins of the people and explain the reason for impending danger. He was there as a reminder that God can still uplift his people; hence, his name 'God has uplifted'.

Jeremiah 28:1-17 (Read)

This story goes a long way to determine why Jeremiah was called. It was a period where people wanted to hear the right things, and not be told of their sins. It was a time when it was fine with them to have idols, and still praise God. We also see a Prophet who will want Israel to be delivered, and see God change His mind about the impending doom.

Jeremiah 31:31-36
The days are coming, declares the Lord, when I will make a

new covenant with the people of Israel and with the people of Judah. It will not be like the covenant I made with their ancestors when I took them by the hand to lead them out of Egypt, because they broke my covenant, though I was a husband to them, declares the Lord. This is the covenant I will make with the people of Israel after that time, declares the Lord. I will put my law in their minds and write it on their hearts. I will be their God, and they will be my people. No longer will they teach their neighbor, or say to one another, Know the Lord,' because they will all know me, from the least of them to the greatest," declares the Lord. For I will forgive their wickedness and will remember their sins no more. This is what the Lord says, he who appoints the sun to shine by day, who decrees the moon and stars to shine by night, who stirs up the sea so that its waves roar, the Lord Almighty is his name: Only if these decrees vanish from my sight, declares the Lord, will Israel ever cease being a nation before me.

From the scriptures you will discover that at one point the prophet must of a necessity declare Gods Judgments, but on the other hand, he has heard of the abundant mercies of God, so here he is hoping and believing. He leaned more on the mercies, rather than the judgment. He had hoped that, though, God said He will deal with Israel, but that He is also a God of Mercy.

However, gradually, it began to look less like what he saw. Rather than the usual mercy he knew, he began to see mercy in a new face: The Face of a Mirage. The Healing, deliverance, began to take the shape of this new face. It looks like deliverance is around the corner, but all of a sudden it disappears.

A mirage is a situation that looks like it is going to happen, but it doesn't happen. In a mirage there is an element embedded in it, it is called frustration. The concept of a mirage is designed to frustrate you. From the scripture we read, Jeremiah waited for the Harvest; he saw the harvest from afar.

Let us go deeper into the word, **Jeremiah 8:20**,
The harvest is past, the summer has ended, and we are not saved.

The harvest is past is a statement of crushed expectations. The summer has ended is a reminder that 'oh, we need to start this all over again.' Do I need to go back to school? Do I need to do that certification? What about the certifications I did before that I have not even worked with? The harvest is past, the summer has ended is a statement of one getting tired of waiting, getting tired of the mirage.

Verse 22 says, *"Is there no balm in Gilead? Is there no physician there? Why then is there no healing for the wound of my people?"*

The face of a mirage disturbed Joseph; the first face of a mirage was when he was thrown into a pit by his brothers. The second face of a mirage was when he was sold into slavery. The third face of a mirage was when he was falsely accused by Mrs. Potiphar, and was thrown into prison. While he was in prison, he saw an opportunity that he thought could deliver him from prison, when he interpreted the Baker's dreams to him, and hoped that the Baker would put in a word for him, but it was a mirage. The bible said the Baker forgot about Joseph, who stayed in that cold prison for another two years.

'Gilead' means Hill of Testimony. You are stepping into the hill of testimony from now. Each step you take brings you closer to the top. You cannot lose hope while climbing the hill of testimony. The Balm has always been in Gilead. The Balm has the ability to heal, but the balm has been dormant for too long; God is calling you to activate that which is dormant. To activate is to make something operative.

Note that Gilead was an area east of the Jordan River, well known for its spices and ointments. In 2kings 5:1-14 Naaman got healed of leprosy in the Jordan. The balm was what healed Naaman at river Jordan. The balm has been sipping into river Jordan; all Naaman needed was to activate this balm. The activation code that was needed to activate this balm was "OBEDIENCE". Some things were standing in the way of the obedience of Naaman: One was pride; two was what looked like a better alternative - Abana and Pharpar, the rivers of Damascus.

Abana and Pharpa are spiritual detours. God wants to change that face of a mirage to a face of certainty. Hope will be restored, goals are about to be met, and you will taste victory again.

Chapter Eleven

The Mind Game

"Mount Gerizim and Mount Ebal became the symbol of blessings and curses."

Tim woke up on the floor of the bathroom close to the toilet. He had no idea how long he had been there and only dim memories of the night before. Everything about his life seemed like a nightmare; and all of it, the whole messy situation with his life seemed to culminate in the emptying of his stomach hours earlier. Why he had allowed it come to this, he had no idea; he had allowed his insecurities build up wrong images in his mind, which he eventually began to act upon, until it finally resulted in the breakdown of his family. But today, he knew one thing for sure; he was done, done with acting out, done with his mind playing games on him, and done with falling for the games. He knew the truth, had known the truth all along, but had allowed the façade to rule.... Not anymore.

The book of Deuteronomy is known as the book of laws. The book consists of three sermons or speeches delivered to the Israelites by Moses on the plains of Moab, shortly before they entered the Promise Land. There are things we are holding on to God for that He has promised us, and just like the Israelite, before you enter into a promise, it is necessary that you know and understand certain things.

As we remind God of His promises, as we hold on to those promises, it is of necessity that we allow God to speak to us and tell us certain things needed in order to claim what He has promised us.

Deuteronomy 11:18-32
Fix these words of mine in your hearts and minds; tie them as symbols on your hands and bind them on your foreheads. Teach them to your children, talking about them when you sit at home and when you walk along the road, when you lie down and when you get up. Write them on the doorframes of your houses and on your gates, so that your days and the days of your children may be many in the land the Lord swore to give your ancestors, as many as the days that the heavens are above the earth. If you carefully observe all these commands I am giving you to follow—to love the Lord your God, to walk in obedience to him and to hold fast to him, then the Lord will drive out all these nations before you, and you will dispossess nations larger and stronger than you. Every place where you set your foot will be yours: Your territory will extend from the desert to Lebanon, and from the Euphrates River to the Mediterranean Sea. No one will be able to stand against you. The Lord your God, as he promised you, will put the terror and fear of you on the whole land, wherever you go. See, I am setting before you today a blessing and a curse, the blessing if you obey the commands of the Lord your God that I am giving you today; the curse if you disobey the commands of theLord

your God and turn from the way that I command you today by following other gods, which you have not known. When the Lord your God has brought you into the land you are entering to possess, you are to proclaim on Mount Gerizim the blessings, and on Mount Ebal the curses. As you know, these mountains are across the Jordan, westward, toward the setting sun, near the great trees of Moreh, in the territory of those Canaanites living in the Arabah in the vicinity of Gilgal. You are about to cross the Jordan to enter and take possession of the land the Lord your God is giving you. When you have taken it over and are living there, be sure that you obey all the decrees and laws I am setting before you today.

The beginning verses referred to those listening to the laws. It was important to those who were listening at that time to get the message, because if there's a misunderstanding of what was told to them, a whole generation could miss it. He wanted the people to fully understand it before passing it on to their generation. It used 'Fix, Tie and bind.' Fix in your hearts and minds.

God used two different places: the Heart and the mind. These are two different compartment areas that hold and control the issues of life. However, I want to focus on one compartment on this topic titled, "The Mind Game".

The Mind is defined as that which observes, learns, and processes what we see, hear, and touch. We react to what the mind has processed

Jeremiah 17:10
I the Lord search the heart and examine the mind, to reward each person according to their conduct, according to what

their deeds deserve.

What do you search for and what do you examine? You search for tangible things and you examine intangible things. The intangible things are more deadly, if not properly taken care of. So motives are embedded in the minds, and desires are embedded in the mind. We have heard or read scriptures about guarding our hearts, but what I think is equally as important is to guard the mind. Moses was preaching one of his sermons in Deuteronomy; he said 'fix these words in your heart and minds'.

There was a reason why he had to mention the mind. As they were listening to the words, the ball will be set in motion, the storage capacity, called the mind is activated. Things begin to happen, the whistle of decision is blown, and the games begin. The mind game starts, which words will prevail, which instructions will be followed, etc. Questions are raised, issues are looked at, and the examination begins. Moses continued with his sermon in Verse 26-32.

Mount Gerizim and Mount Ebal became the symbol of blessings and curses. There is a pull from Gerizim for us to choose the blessings, and there is a pull from Ebal to go the way of curses, but the issue is that the curses may not be labeled as curses, so we may not know, just like the bible rightly says, *'there is a way that seems right to a man, but he does not know that it is the way of destruction'*. However, God being a wise God has given us what will help us win this mind game.

Taking the wrong turn is almost a pattern for the impatient Israelites, no wonder Joshua said, *"choose this day whom you will serve, as for me and my house we will serve the Lord"*. Do you want to go the way of Gerizim or the way of Ebal? The way of Gerizim and the way of Ebal becomes a mind game. Anytime we make up our minds, we have decided to stay at either Gerizim or Ebal.

Paul was addressing the Philippian church, and he discovered that the church was entangled in a mind game. The church was torn between mount Gerizim and mount Ebal. He knew that even though they were in the New Testament, they were still stuck, confused, and constantly fighting battles in their minds, between Gerizim and Ebal. Like some of us, we are still trying to make up our minds on certain moral issues, business issues, and life issues. Every one of us, like the Philippian church, goes through this mind game. God is speaking to us through the same words that Paul told the church

Philipians 4:8-9
Finally, brethren, whatsoever things are true, whatsoever things are honest, whatsoever things are just, whatsoever things are pure, whatsoever things are lovely, whatsoever things are of good report; if there be any virtue, and if there be any praise, think on these things. Whatever you have learned or received or heard from me, or seen in me, put it into practice. And the God of peace will be with you.

Verse 8 becomes the guiding principle when involved in a mind game. The listed anchors, which now becomes directional arrows are:
1. True
2. Honest

3. Just
4. Pure
5. Lovely

Most importantly, there must be virtue and excellence. Think on these things; meditate on them.

A brief background: From the letters Paul wrote to the Corinthian church.

2Corinthians 11:24
Five times I received from the Jews the forty lashes minus one. Three times I was beaten with rods, once I was stoned, three times I was shipwrecked, I spent a night and a day in the open sea, I have been constantly on the move. I have been in danger from rivers, in danger from bandits, in danger from my own countrymen, in danger from Gentiles; in danger in the city, in danger in the country, in danger at sea; and in danger from false brothers. I have labored and toiled and have often gone without sleep; I have known hunger and thirst and have often gone without food; I have been cold and naked.

This was the life of Paul; but then he writes a most profound letter:

Philippians 4:4
Rejoice in the Lord always. I will say it again: Rejoice!

What makes a man that passed through all these, get to a place where he says, "rejoice in the Lord?" Think on these things' is a reminder to think on the right things. The negativity and depression that may have erupted from the church may have started getting to Paul; the mind game that started in the lives of the Philippians may have triggered a mind game in Paul, and he had to nip it in the bud before it takes root in him, with the statement, 'Rejoice in the Lord always!'

Are you going through a mind game? Is your mind playing tricks on you? You are the reason for this Word. Paul was going through some difficult times, his reactions could easily have been: Why is this happening to me? Why is God allowing this? What good am I doing God, and the Kingdom work when I am in jail? But no, he ordered himself to rejoice in the Lord, and took control of his mind. He understood the game had started, he considered that someone amongst them might be battling the same issues, so he took his pen and decided to write them a letter to encourage them, while also encouraging himself.

Paul is simply saying to us that when the negative things get overwhelming, when it looks like God is far away, and you feel like you are alone, just like he felt alone, think on these life-enriching things.

Chapter Twelve

Beyond Knowledge

"The greatest enemy of knowledge is not ignorance, it is the illusion of knowledge" – Stephen Hawking

From the back of the church, Tim felt like a man who had just had his sight adjusted. The sermon was strong; pointing out the truth that God is not only our Savior and Lord, but also the Almighty One, who chose to love us with everlasting love, and wants us to know Him deeper than we do, so that we can discover and live the life He has planned for us; a God to be held in awe. So gripping were Pastor Pete's words that all other thoughts had been pushed from Tim's mind; and now with his heart broken wide open by the message, he knew that was a good thing. He still did not know why God had chosen this morning to get his attention after his many years of mediocre faith, but he knew without a doubt, he was here for a reason, as if he had shown up for a divine appointment to truly get to know Him, rather than living with the illusion of knowing Him.

Paul wrote a letter to the Ephesian Christians about a revealed mystery.

Ephesians 3:6-7
That the Gentiles should be fellow heirs, of the same body, and partakers of His promise in Christ through the gospel, of which I became a minister according to the gift of the grace of God given to me by the effective working of His power.

The salient words are Gentiles, Heirs and Partakers of his promise, which means that a group of people that were not originally counted as heirs, that have not come from the Jewish lineage, and that have been looked down upon for generations, are now suddenly identified as heirs. The word 'Gentiles' means the nations, and all those that are not of the house of Israel.

In **Ephesians 3:9-13**, Paul talks about the Purpose of the Mystery:
And to make all see what is the fellowship of the mystery, which from the beginning of the ages has been hidden in God who created all things through Jesus Christ; to the intent that now the manifold wisdom of God might be made known by the church to the principalities and powers in the heavenly places, according to the eternal purpose which He accomplished in Christ Jesus our Lord, in whom we have boldness and access with confidence through faith in Him. Therefore I ask that you do not lose heart at my tribulations for you, which is your glory.

From **Verse 14-19**, there was an appreciation of this mystery, and a prayer was said on behalf of the Ephesians:
For this reason I bow my knees to the Father of our Lord Jesus Christ, from whom the whole family in heaven and earth is named, that He would grant you, according to the

riches of His glory, to be strengthened with might through His Spirit in the inner man, that Christ may dwell in your hearts through faith; that you, being rooted and grounded in love, may be able to comprehend with all the saints what is the width and length and depth and height, to know the love of Christ which passes knowledge; that you may be filled with all the fullness of God.

We see a mystery revealed, this mystery for Paul, is that the gentiles can be partakers of His Promise. This mystery revealed is how you and I can partake of God's promises. This mystery is saying it does not matter where you are coming from, your future can be bright; it is saying it does not matter how many times you have prayed about the issue, God can still make a way for you. It is saying, though you have received a report, but that report does not define you.

After the revelation of this mystery, the purpose of the mystery is known. The blessings are highlighted; then the actual manifestation will come, based on the prayers that Paul prayed for the Ephesians in Verse 3:16-19, *"that He would grant you, according to the riches of His glory, to be strengthened with might through His Spirit in the inner man, that Christ may dwell in your hearts through faith; that you, being rooted and grounded in love, may be able to comprehend with all the saints what is the width and length and depth and height, to know the love of Christ which passes knowledge; that you may be filled with all the fullness of God."*

God is calling us to a deeper knowledge. This deeper knowledge is what Paul prayed for the Ephesians. This deeper knowledge is what made Paul to stay at Ephesus, despite seeing a great and effectual door in front of him that had many adversaries on both sides. This deeper knowledge is what Brother James was talking about when he said, "count it all joy when you fall into diverse trials."

"The greatest enemy of knowledge is not ignorance, it is the illusion of knowledge." — Stephen Hawking. These words are so true and profound, for when you think you know, and in reality you don't know, it is more dangerous for you, than when you do not know at all, when you are ignorant. So, how do we get to this avenue called "beyond knowledge?"

You don't only read the Word, but you meditate and stay on the Word. How long you stay on a promise will determine how quickly you get the promise.

John 1:1-14
In the beginning was the Word, and the Word was with God, and the Word was God. He was in the beginning with God. All things came into being through Him, and apart from Him nothing came into being that has come into being. In Him was life, and the life was the Light of men. The Light shines in the darkness, and the darkness did not comprehend it. And the Word became flesh, and dwelt among us, and we saw His glory, glory as of the only begotten from the Father, full of grace and truth. There came a man sent from God, whose name was John. He came as a witness, to testify about the Light, so that all might believe through him. He was not the Light, but he came to testify about the Light. There was the true Light which, coming into the world, enlightens every man. He was in the world, and the world was made through Him, and the

world did not know Him. He came to His own, and those who were His own did not receive Him. But as many as received Him, to them He gave the right to become children of God, even to those who believe in His name, who were born, not of blood nor of the will of the flesh nor of the will of man, but of God. And the Word became flesh, and dwelt among us, and we saw His glory, glory as of the only begotten from the Father, full of grace and truth

Although John was talking about the birth of Jesus, this scripture reveals much more than what John was saying. This scripture is telling us that as we stay on the Word, as we meditate on the Word, as we reference the Word, there will be times when this Word will no longer be words, this Word will become flesh, which means it becomes what you see and feel, it becomes a manifestation of that which you have asked of God.

****

In the Time of the Latter Rain

"The latter rain is the rain that will surely come just before the harvest."

Zechariah 10:1-12 (Read)

For us to talk about the later rain, there must of a necessity be a former rain. The later rain may not be beneficial unless we have received a former rain. The former rain represents the grace, you as a believer in Jesus Christ, first received to help your seed germinate and grow. The former rain is enough to start you growing up as a child of God. The former rain is the initial deposit God gives us to invest.

I believe that how you handle your former rain will go a long way to determine how you activate or utilize your latter rain. If we don't recognize when the latter rain falls, we begin to struggle to achieve certain things in life.

John 5:1-15
After these things there was a feast of the Jews, and Jesus went up to Jerusalem. Now there is in Jerusalem by the sheep gate a pool, which is called in Hebrew Bethesda, having five porticoes. In these lay a multitude of those who were sick, blind, lame, and withered, [waiting for the moving of the waters; for an angel of the Lord went down at certain seasons into the pool and stirred up the water; whoever then first, after the stirring up of the water, stepped in was made well from whatever disease with which he was afflicted.] A man was there who had been ill for thirty-eight years. When Jesus saw him lying there, and knew that he had already been a long time in that condition, He said to him, "Do you wish to get well?" The sick man answered Him, "Sir, I have no man to put me into the pool when the water is stirred up, but while I am coming, another steps down before me. Jesus said to him, Get up, pick up your pallet and walk. Immediately the man became well, and picked up his pallet and began to walk. Now it was the Sabbath on that day. So the Jews were saying to the man who was cured, it is the Sabbath, and it is not permissible for you to carry your pallet. But he answered them, He who made me well was the one who said to me, 'Pick up your pallet and walk. They asked him, Who is the man who said to you, 'Pick up your pallet and walk'? But the man who was

healed did not know who it was, for Jesus had slipped away while there was a crowd in that place. Afterward Jesus found him in the temple and said to him, "Behold, you have become well; do not sin anymore, so that nothing worse happens to you. The man went away, and told the Jews that it was Jesus who had made him well

These people that have been sitting by the pool represent you and I. They represent what we believe God for. There are things we have been waiting for: Some of us have been waiting to get married, waiting to have a child, waiting to get promoted, waiting to get healed. How many times have you believed that the next promotion was going to be yours, and all of a sudden, they give it to someone else? You are still waiting by the water.

An angel goes down to the pool a certain season, which means that the season may not even be consistent, so many of them just stay by the pool hoping that it will be when they are ready that the water will be troubled.

'A certain season' represents chance, so you may even be the strongest amongst the sick, but if you are not paying attention to when the water is stirred, you will have to wait till next year. 'A certain season' tells me that some will do whatever possible to cheat or find a way to hinder other people. The healing they received once a year was the former rain. The setting of this man that was at the pool was significant. Here, God was showing us that people who are preaching the Word have started getting used to the former rain. We now look forward to mercy drops, instead of asking for showers. The former rain can only do a little bit at certain times; it can get you healed only every once in a while.

Zechariah 10:1
Ask ye of the LORD rain in the time of the latter rain; so the LORD shall make bright clouds, and give them showers of rain, to every one grass in the field.

Deuteronomy 11:14
That I will give you the rain of your land in his due season, the first rain and the latter rain, that thou mayest gather in thy corn, and thy wine, and thine oil.

Job 29:23
And they waited for me as for the rain; and they opened their mouth wide as for the latter rain.

Hosea 6:3
Then shall we know, if we follow on to know the LORD: his going forth is prepared as the morning; and he shall come unto us as the rain, as the latter and former rain unto the earth.

Take a look at something significant about the pool by the sheep gate: An Angel was responsible for the troubling of the water for only one person to be healed per season. While this man and so many others were struggling to get a piece of the former rain, the later rain personified- Jesus, showed up, and the man almost missed it, because he was focusing so much on the former rain. The Latter Rain is the rain that will surely come just before the

Harvest, expect it and focus on it, so you can recognize it when it pours down.

Chapter Thirteen

The Rearview Mirror
"The things of old started as former things"

Tim smiled, reminiscing on God's word about doing a new thing in his life. Just a year ago, he was a wreck; he looked back at his life, and couldn't believe how far he has come. He had lost all hope, his situation had degenerated so badly, he couldn't even recognize himself then; and how reality finally dawned on him on his bathroom floor, with his face in the toilet bowl, after a night of usual drunkenness; and how God had pulled him out of all that mess, and restored all to him. Overwhelmed with gratitude, he mouthed a heartfelt thanks to God for the new thing He had begun in his life.

Numbers 11:1-8 (Read)

Isaiah 43:18-19
do not remember the former things, Nor consider the things of old. Behold, I will do a new thing, now it shall spring forth; shall you not know it? I will even make a road in the wilderness and rivers in the desert.

The rear view mirror is a mirror placed in cars that helps us to see what is behind us as we drive along. The same way we have a rearview mirror in our cars, we also have spiritual rearview mirrors. The spiritual rearview mirrors can be used for two purposes:

* The first Purpose of a spiritual rearview mirror is to reflect on what God did for us in the past to enable us look towards the future with great expectations. Based on this principle, back in the bible days, when God did something spectacular for His children, He will ask His people to establish a memorial. Why did God tell them to establish a memorial? Why will God ask them to do something that they will not forget easily? The reason is simple, when we look through the rearview mirror, these memorials stand out, and it gives us encouragement, it tells us that God is still in the business of miracles.

* The second use of the rearview mirror is that, we tend to see the former things and things of old. The former things can be defined as what used to be the norm. The things of old started as former things. The things of old become long-standing problems, and can easily become a belief system. So when we look at the rearview mirror, we are only being reminded of the former things and things of old. The former things and the things of old can also blind us from seeing the new things ahead.

In **Numbers 11**, God was taking His people to a new place. These people had no idea what it was going to be like in the new place. The same way God said, "I'm doing a new thing"; some of us may not be fully aware of what this new thing will be like. The people heard when

God spoke to Moses, and everyone said 'amen' when the word was declared. Moses told everyone to jump into the bus to a new destination. Has Moses been there before? No.

Exodus 14:10-12
Verse 10: *As Pharaoh approached, the Israelites looked up, and there were the Egyptians, marching after them. They were terrified and cried out to the LORD.*
As they were moving towards the new place they looked at the rear view mirror, and they saw the Egyptians approaching; that terrified them. As you look at the rear view mirror, you see the symptoms coming back, we have declared that the balm is in Gilead, but you still feel the pain, because we are looking at the rear view mirror.

Verse 11-12: *They said to Moses, "Was it because there were no graves in Egypt that you brought us to the desert to die? What have you done to us by bringing us out of Egypt? Didn't we say to you in Egypt, 'Leave us alone; let us serve the Egyptians'? It would have been better for us to serve the Egyptians than to die in the desert!"*

As you try to stay focused and believe God for a new thing, there will be times when you have to look at the rearview mirror. Someone is looking at the rearview mirror right now, and what you are seeing is not encouraging, you may be terrified, and comparing where you were then with where you are now, like the Israelites compared what they saw to their former situation in Egypt. The rearview mirror came in front of them at a crucial time, the rearview mirror made them beg to be slaves all over again. God is saying to you, 'see my goodness'. Change your perspective of 'I will do a new thing', to 'I AM DOING A NEW THING'.

****

Riding on the Wings of Hope
"Hope is being able to see that there is light, despite all the darkness" – Desmond Tutu

Romans 8:22-25(MSG)
All around us we observe a pregnant creation. The difficult times of pain throughout the world are simply birth pangs. But it's not only around us; it's within us. The Spirit of God is arousing us within. We're also feeling the birth pangs. These sterile and barren bodies of ours are yearning for full deliverance. That is why waiting does not diminish us, any more than waiting diminishes a pregnant mother. We are enlarged in the waiting. We, of course, don't see what is enlarging us. But the longer we wait, the larger we become, and the more joyful our expectancy.

As we hold on to hope, there is restoration, there is healing, there is joy. All these ties to the truth that God is doing a new thing. The big question is why do we need to ride on the wings of hope?

The Biblical definition of hope is trust, to expect and anticipate with pleasure

Psalm 39:7
And now, Lord, what wait I for? my hope is in thee.

Colossians 1:5
For the hope which is laid up for you in heaven, whereof ye heard before in the word of the truth of the gospel;

At a time like this, we must of a necessity leave the general definition of hope that we may know, and hang on to the biblical definition of hope. We must depart from what we know as hope to what the bible calls hope. The word for you today is 'Hope'. God is telling you to trust, and anticipate with pleasure.

When hope is activated, a few things have to change: business is no longer as usual; and the state that you were once comfortable in, is no longer a comfortable state.

1 Kings 18:1-18
After a long time, in the third year, the word of the Lord came to Elijah: Go and present yourself to Ahab, and I will send rain on the land. So Elijah went to present himself to Ahab. Now the famine was severe in Samaria, and Ahab had summoned Obadiah, his palace administrator. (Obadiah was a devout believer in the Lord. While Jezebel was killing off the Lord's prophets, Obadiah had taken a hundred prophets and hidden them in two caves, fifty in each, and had supplied them with food and water.) Ahab had said to Obadiah, "Go through the land to all the springs and valleys. Maybe we can find some grass to keep the horses and mules alive so we will not have to kill any of our animals." So they divided the land they were to cover, Ahab going in one direction and Obadiah in another. As Obadiah was walking along, Elijah met him. Obadiah recognized him, bowed down to the ground, and said, "Is it really you, my lord Elijah? "Yes," he replied. Go tell your mas-

ter, Elijah is here. What have I done wrong, asked Obadiah, that you are handing your servant over to Ahab to be put to death? As surely as the Lord your God lives, there is not a nation or kingdom where my master has not sent someone to look for you. And whenever a nation or kingdom claimed you were not there, he made them swear they could not find you. But now you tell me to go to my master and say, 'Elijah is here.' I don't know where the Spirit of the Lord may carry you when I leave you. If I go and tell Ahab and he doesn't find you, he will kill me. Yet I your servant have worshiped the Lord since my youth. Haven't you heard, my lord, what I did while Jezebel was killing the prophets of the Lord? I hid a hundred of the Lord's prophets in two caves, fifty in each, and supplied them with food and water. And now you tell me to go to my master and say, 'Elijah is here.' He will kill me! Elijah said, As the Lord Almighty lives, whom I serve, I will surely present myself to Ahab today. So Obadiah went to meet Ahab and told him, and Ahab went to meet Elijah. When he saw Elijah, he said to him, "Is that you, you troubler of Israel? I have not made trouble for Israel, Elijah replied. But you and your father's family have. You have abandoned the Lord's commands and have followed the Baals.

"It came to pass after many days..." How long have you been in that unpleasant situation? How much have you lost since you stepped into that issue? The people of God and the Prophet Elijah found themselves in a state after many days. The state you find yourself could be many months or years. However, after many days, there came an arrival of the Word. What the Word was telling the Prophet was contrary to what they were feeling at that time. What you have heard concerning that situation may be contrary to what you are currently feeling, but it doesn't change the truth.

God told Elijah, "go present yourself to the king who is in charge of the kingdom, where you are currently staying, as *I will do a new thing*"

The carrier of the Word of deliverance came through the Prophet, and Obadiah recognized him. Do you know how many times we have walked past someone important to our destiny, or refused to do something that can help us? Do you know how many good things have passed you by, because you couldn't recognize them or you were too afraid to pay attention?

Now, it is time to ride on the wings of hope, for all that you have desired of the Lord. Go present yourself to the Lord, the set time has come for you, be expectant with joy, it is a new day, and God is doing a new thing.

Epilogue

The Power of Gratitude

"Bless the Lord O my soul; and all that is within me, Bless His holy name!"

Thanksgiving day is a great reminder that we need to cultivate an attitude of gratitude, a heart that appreciates the goodness of God, especially with the way Paul described the last days.

2 Timothy 3:2-4
For men will be lovers of themselves, lovers of money, boasters, proud, blasphemers, disobedient to parents, unthankful, unholy, unloving, unforgiving, slanderers, without self-control, brutal, despisers of good, traitors, headstrong, haughty, lovers of pleasure, rather than lovers of God.

Let's pay attention to one of the characteristics mentioned right in the middle of the list of wrongs, which is being "unthankful" or "ungrateful." We can miss great blessings, because we are ungrateful; and we can miss heaven, because of the sin of being unthankful, which is an expression of dissatisfaction, or discontent.

One of the primary ways that ingratitude manifests itself is in complaining and murmuring. Remember the Israelites in the wilderness, who didn't appreciate all that God had done for them, but rather grumbled and complained about everything; hence, that entire generation was eventually wiped out, and prevented from entering the promise land.

Psalm 103:1-5
Bless the LORD, O my soul; And all that is within me, bless His holy name! Bless the LORD, O my soul, and forget not all His benefits: Who forgives all your iniquities, who heals all your diseases, Who redeems your life from destruction, who crowns you with loving-kindness and tender mercies, Who satisfies your mouth with good things, So that your youth is renewed like the eagle's.

David compelled his soul to bless the Lord, to appreciate the Lord. 'All that is within him' means all that belongs to him and all that is in him must not forget all God's benefits, not some of His benefits, or benefits that can be seen in our outlook, or in our bank accounts. Forget not the big things, the little things, and even those things that are in the pipeline right now. Forget not how He pulled you out of the miry clay. Forget not how he delivered you from that accident. Forget not how he rescued you from people you called your friends, but are wolves in sheep clothing. Forget not how God forgave your sins. Forget not how He healed you from that sickness that you thought would kill you. Forget not the one that crowns you with loving kindness and tender mercies. Forget not the one that satisfies your mouth with good things so that your youth is renewed - divine health. We might have occasional headaches here and there, but what we have is constant divine health. There are so many reasons to be thankful.

Cicero once said, *"A thankful heart is not only the greatest virtue, but the parent of all other virtues."*

William A. Ward said *"God gave you a gift of 86,400 seconds today. Have you used one second to say "thank you?"*

The story of the infamous nine is so poignant:

Luke 17:11-19
Now on his way to Jerusalem, Jesus traveled along the border between Samaria and Galilee. As he was going into a village, ten men who had leprosy met him. They stood at a distance and called out in a loud voice, "Jesus, Master, have pity on us!" When he saw them, he said, "Go, show yourselves to the priests." And as they went, they were cleansed. One of them, when he saw he was healed, came back, praising God in a loud voice. He threw himself at Jesus' feet and thanked him, and he was a Samaritan. Jesus asked, "Were not all ten cleansed? Where are the other nine? Has no one returned to give praise to God except this foreigner? Then he said to him, "Rise and go; your faith has made you well.

Jesus was traveling along the border between Samaria and Galilee, and met people who are in the border of life, who are outcasts, because they were leprous, they could not stay amongst healthy people in the towns. They had lost their jobs and homes, sleeping outside during winter and summer; they had to scavenge for food to survive; they had limitations, because of their health. However, Jesus shows up one day and healed their bodies. The priest restored them back to the community.

You would think the story would end there, but then the bible goes on to tell us that only one of the nine of them healed, came back to say thank you. This simple act of gratitude earned the man something more that the other nine missed out on, Jesus declared to him that his faith has made him whole; this means full restoration of his wellbeing, and all that he needs to have a good life.

No matter what is going on with you right now, be thankful, that is the one assured way to stay on the path of growth, and keep the seed of life growing sustainably, in season and out of season.

www.ingramcontent.com/pod-product-compliance
Lightning Source LLC
LaVergne TN
LVHW051559070426
835507LV00021B/2671